Y0-EGH-302

THE BEST OF THE
JOB
GODDESS

Phenomenal Job Search Advice From The Country's Most Popular Legal Job Search Columnist

KIMM ALAYNE WALTON, J.D.

Harcourt Brace Legal & Professional Publications, Inc.
Editorial Offices: 111 West Jackson Boulevard,
7th Floor, Chicago, IL 60604
Regional Offices: Chicago, Dallas, Los Angeles,
New York, Washington, D.C.

Distributed by:
Harcourt Brace and Company
6277 Sea Harbor Drive, Orlando, FL 32887-6777
Phone: 1-800-787-8717
Fax: 1-800-433-6303

Copyright © 1999 by Harcourt Brace Legal & Professional Publications, Inc. All rights reserved. No part of this publication may be reproduced or transmitted in any form or by any means, electronic or mechanical, including photocopying, recording, or any information storage or retrieval system, without permission in writing from the publisher.

Requests for permission to make copies of any part of the work should be mailed to: Harcourt Brace Legal & Professional Publications, Inc., Attention: Customer Service Department, 6277 Sea Harbor Drive, Orlando, FL 32887-6777.

Printed in the United States of America.

Permissions: The image of Venus on the cover is a detail from Sandro Botticelli's *Venus and Mars*, c. 1483, Panel (69.2 x 173.4 cm), © The National Gallery, London.

Cover Design: Robert Aulicino/Pro-Art Graphic Design (Prescott, Arizona)
Interior Design: Desktop Miracles (Dallas, Texas)

HARCOURT BRACE
Legal & Professional Publications, Inc.

THE **barbri** GROUP

Harcourt Brace Legal & Professional Publications offers a variety of products and services for professionals, including Gilbert Law Summaries, Legalines, and Bar/Bri Bar Review. For a complete listing of products and services visit Harcourt Brace on the Web at www.gilbertlaw.com, or contact: Harcourt Brace Legal & Professional Publications, Inc., 111 West Jackson Boulevard, 7th Floor, Chicago, IL 60604. Phone: 1-800-782-1272. Fax: 1-312-360-1842.

Table of Contents

Acknowledgments

If you're at all familiar with the Job Goddess column, you know that the Job Goddess doesn't fly solo. All of the Job Goddess's advice comes from the tremendously knowledgeable people who are quoted in virtually every answer the Job Goddess gives. To my wonderful, accessible pool of experts: A million thanks.

I must also thank John Mastandrea. He not only funneled many of the Job Goddess questions in this book to me, but he also has a very wry and funny take on life that makes his missives all the more entertaining. And Stephanie Kartofels has yet again taken a simple manuscript and made it look breathtaking. Stef, I may be the Goddess, but you're the magician.

No acknowledgment section for any of my books would be complete without mentioning my brother Keir, a constant source of encouragement, ideas—and noodges where necessary!

And of course there would be no Job Goddess at all if there weren't questions to answer, and for those questions I must thank the many, many law school students and graduates who send along their concerns. The great Albert Schweitzer once said that the only people who would be happy in life are those who help others. So if you think the Job Goddess is doing you the favor with advice on job searches—it's really the other way around, and I'm very grateful.

Kimm Alayne Walton
Wilton, Connecticut

This book is dedicated to

my wonderful fiancé, Henry—

a constant reminder to me that it's not the stuff

you've got in your life that counts, but the people.

I may not really be a goddess, but Sweetheart,

you make me feel like one.

Introduction

When I wrote the book *Guerrilla Tactics for Getting the Legal Job of Your Dreams*, I thought, jeez, this book is 550 pages long. I must have covered everything any law student could possibly want to know about getting a job!

Of course—I hadn't. And that was brought home to me when I started visiting law schools around the country, and students peppered me with questions I hadn't covered in *Guerrilla Tactics*. It was that experience that gave me the inspiration to start "Job Goddessing."

From the start, I only had one rule with the Job Goddess column. Okay, actually two rules. One was that it had to be funny as well as helpful, because I think boring-ness is just the worst possible sin. But more importantly, I was bound and determined that the Job Goddess would never say never. Sometimes the situations my correspondents describe seem incredibly bleak ("I've failed the Bar three times. Now what?"). But having spoken with thousands of law students, graduates, employers, and career counselors all over the country, I'm convinced that there is *no* fatal flaw, nothing that prevents anybody from finding a career that will make them happy. Nothing. And the Job Goddess column reflects that philosophy.

And even though the advice the Job Goddess dispenses seems light-hearted, it *works*. I know that if only because the experts I quote have seen it all, and counseled law students and graduates through all kinds of job search obstacles. The Job Goddess doesn't herself have any particular expertise, but she does have the divine good judgment to rely on people who *do*.

This book gives you a pretty comprehensive grab-bag of Job Goddess columns. No matter what you think is standing between you and your dream job, I'm sure you'll find at least a few columns that'll speak to you. If you'd like to see more of the Job Goddess, you can reach it through the Gilbert's home page, at Gilbertlaw.com. And if you like, you can send questions to me directly. My e-mail address is jobgoddess@aol.com. I don't have the chance to respond to every query, but I do my best!

Eternally Yours,

Kimm Alayne Walton
a/k/a The Job Goddess

I-I-I…Don't Wanna Be a Lifeguard

Summer Jobs

How Do I Get a Summer Job After My First Year in Law School?

Dear Job Goddess,

Help! I am a first-year student looking for practical legal experience over the summer. I had no idea how hard it would be to find a good job—it seems that 1Ls are rarely considered. Do you have any advice regarding what I can do to stand out from every other 1L looking for work? What options should I consider?

GB, Boston

Dear Job Goddess,

My girlfriend is in her first year at a tier-one law school and is trying to find a position with a law firm for the summer. She is having no luck at all even though her grades and class rank are great. What can we do?

MJ, Illinois

Dear Job Goddess,

I have been in law school for one semester, and I am trying to decide what I should do next summer. I thought I would pursue a law clerk position at a law firm, but of the 100+ resumes I have sent out, I have had two interviews and no offers. Most of the employers I wrote to didn't even respond. Now what?

EG, New York

Dear GB, MJ, and EG,

The Job Goddess applauds all of you for hitting the legal career ground running. Why, when she was in your shoes, in her pre-Goddess incarnation, the Job Goddess was thinking, "If I max out my credit cards, can I spend the summer in Egypt?" You, of course, not only have the right instincts, but also the divine guidance of the Job Goddess's pool of experts. You will be delighted to know that, approached strategically, your first law school summer can launch your legal career into the stratosphere.

How? The important point to remember about your first summer is *not* to focus on what your classmates will focus on—that is, getting a paying position with as large a law firm as possible. There are at least three reasons not to do this. One is that unless you go to one of the tiny handful of schools whose first-year students are sought by large firms—you know, the "H" school, and the "Y" school, and a few others—you will quickly frustrate yourself by trying to break into their traditional summer clerkship programs. The Job Goddess does not want you to be frustrated; she wants you to be happy and fulfilled. Another, more important reason is that you can get broader experience and much more versatility from other kinds of employers than you can from large firms.

Where *should* you look, the Job Goddess hears you asking? Your happiest hunting grounds are likely to be small firms and judicial internships; of those two, a judicial internship is likely to open the most doors for you. As you undoubtedly know, there are about a bajillion courts, between the federal court system, states, municipal courts, and specialty courts. All of them have judges, and judges all need clerks. As you know, the Job Goddess does not advise you simply to send out mass mailers. Instead, check with your career services director for alumni who are judges, and/or any judges

5

who routinely hire first-year summer associates from your school. Kitty Cooney Hoye, Career Services Director at Notre Dame Law School, points out that "Judicial internships are wonderful no matter what you intend to do after school. They impress law firms, governmental employers, and public interest groups." While your experience from judge to judge will vary, you'll undoubtedly get to research and sit in on a number of cases, which most students really enjoy. Donna Gerson, Assistant Career Services Director at the University of Pittsburgh Law School (and herself a former federal judicial clerk) points out that you also get "A measure of deference new lawyers don't even get, because other lawyers will associate you with the judge." And on top of all of that, Kitty Hoye adds that you'll "Wind up with a great writing sample, and a judge's reference," both of which will be a real boon to your job search later on.

The downside? Most summer judicial clerkships are volunteer positions, and the Job Goddess knows how you cringe at the word "volunteer." However, the experience is so great and will grease the nubile wheels of your career so well that she encourages you to follow Kitty Hoye's advice, and "volunteer 20 to 25 hours a week, if that's all you can afford, and get a paying job with the rest of your time." You would not be the first law student to spend a few hours a week waitering.

The other target the Job Goddess recommends for you is to work with a small firm. "What's so super about a summer job with a small firm?" you ask. You will typically get a lot more responsibility than you would with a larger employer; in fact, you may well get responsibility and client contact that large firm associates don't get for years.

How do you get these small firm jobs? With small firms, timing is everything; they won't hire you for summer jobs the previous fall, the way large firms do, because they won't typically know whether they need anybody that far in advance. But to position yourself for when the fruit is ripe, Kitty Cooney Hoye recommends that you "Go to local bar association meetings in the Spring. A student membership is cheap! These meetings are a great opportunity to see who is doing what, and to let them see you in a non-interview-pressurized situation."

Kitty Hoye also urges you to let your career services director know what you're looking for. "Most first years think that career services isn't there for them," she says. "It's not true! There are a lot of great jobs that are handed down from upperclasspeople to students behind them. The career services office is a great place to find out about those jobs, because they usually hear about them first."

Whether it's a judicial internship or a small firm you decide to pursue, the Job Goddess urges you not to overlook the most direct way to a summer job: research who's who, and then go knocking on doors. Yes, it takes some nerve, but the Job Goddess has never known of a law student to go unemployed for more than a week if they were willing to pound the pavement and overlook a few "nays" in the process. In fact, the Job Goddess knows a third year law student, at a not-Harvard law school, who got two—count 'em, two—summer clerkships with federal trial level judges by showing up the first week of summer vacation, knocking on the right door, and asking if they needed any additional help. As this story illustrates, judges sometimes underestimate how much of a workload they will have—and sometimes their clerks don't work out, or worse, they don't show up at all. The lesson here is that you must never, *ever* count yourself out of a job you'll enjoy.

So set aside your dreams of big bucks from a law job next summer. Put in some time with a judge or a small firm, doing work you'll love, and wait tables to pull in cash if you need to. The Job Goddess assures you that there is no better start to the legal career that you want—and *deserve*—for getting such a head start!

ETERNALLY YOURS,

The Job Goddess

Are Summer Abroad Programs Good for My Career?

Dear Job Goddess,

I'm a 1L. There are tons of posters up at school advertising summer abroad programs. They all tend to imply that this is a smart career move. But because I am in law school I am learning to be a skeptic, so I'm curious. Is a summer abroad something that law firms really like to see on a resume?

BV, Georgia

Dear BV,

Ah, yes. You can picture it now, can't you, BV? The Eiffel Tower. The Musee d'Orsay. The charming little café on the Rive Gauche, the outdoor table where Ernest Hemingway once sat, and where you now picture yourself, coffee in one hand, *petit four* in the other . . . and your International Trade Regulations textbook open on the wrought-iron table in front of you.

There is no question that summer abroad programs have a lot going for them, in terms of life experience. *Vraiment!* But the Job Goddess unfortunately can't ignore that pesky job search thing. So let's see how your scholarly wanderlust plays in the minds of potential employers. Be advised up front, BV, that the Job Goddess will ultimately tell you how to satisfy your urge to flee and advance your career as well, because as you know, the Job Goddess *never* lets you down.

Let's start with the positive job search impact of a summer abroad, shall we? Most obviously, if you have your heart set on working in a particular country, spending not just summers but every possible moment in that country is a good idea. If this is the case, BV, you need to make the most of your time in the country. For one thing, consider a summer program that combines classes with an actual, working internship. The summer abroad program that Syracuse University offers has just such a feature, for instance. Also, take advantage of the time before you go abroad to make as many contacts there as possible. Whether it's through alumni, professors who might have lived in the country you desire, or via the country's embassy, state what you're looking for and who you might talk to while you're over there. You want to sink as many claws into the country by way of meeting the locals as you possibly can. You may also check in the reference section of your library for companies with offices or plants in the country where you want to wind up, and find out if you can work—on a volunteer basis, probably—for them while you're over there. Another option is to take an internship in the American Embassy in your chosen country, which you can find out about through the Foreign Service in Washington, D.C.

The point here is, BV, that while everybody else in the program might use their off-hours to prowl the pubs or beaches, you're going to have to use them for career benefit if you want to make your summer program work for you as much as it can. As you've undoubtedly noticed, the real value of what the Job Goddess is suggesting is not in the summer program itself, but annexed to it. Working for a company or a U.S. Embassy in the country where you'd like to be would be excellent experience without ever having to open up a musty textbook while you're there—and you'd be saving money, to boot.

Even if you have no interest in working in the country you plan to visit, summers abroad have other pluses. One is that employers are always happy—nay, grateful—to see interesting things on your resume, because they're frequently as stumped as you are for things to talk about in interviews. An Amazon-Cruise-And-Advanced-Civil-Procedure-Clinic certainly fits that bill, as would any international program. Travel is simply very easy to talk about, and so it gives you interview fodder.

On top of that, if you are ever going to do a summer program, you're wise to consider it for your first summer in law school. Why is that? Because while employers expect you to spend your second summer getting work experience, there are no similar expectations for your first summer. So if Australia beckons, BV, the time to say g'day and throw a shrimp on the barbie is this summer—not the next one.

And finally, summers abroad are a good opportunity to knock out a few credits, to free up your time during the school year to do some career-oriented work. For instance, if taking six credits during the summer gives you the chance to take on a 20-hour-a-week job working for a judge or a law firm when you get home, you've done yourself quite a favor indeed. Of course, that takes discipline, BV—the temptation will be to use that extra 20 hours to familiarize yourself with the Happy Hour buffet at bars near school, and the Job Goddess trusts that you can overcome that temptation.

Right now you're wondering, BV, why the Job Goddess hasn't told you to fire up your passport and start packing. Here's why. The fact is that if you want a job in this country—be it with the government, or a law firm, or in public interest, or with a corporation—and on top of that you're willing to *spend* money instead of *make* money for a summer, then the Job Goddess has far more productive ways for you to spend your summer than by jetting off to Europe. In a recent column, the Job Goddess praised two kinds of jobs for first years in particular—volunteer judicial clerkships and jobs with small firms. Either of these would get you far, far ahead in the job search game, BV, both in terms of experience and professional contacts. Grades, resumes, and every other law student worry diminishes dramatically if you take the Job Goddess's advice on how to spend your fledgling summer in law school.

Furthermore, if you want to work in international law but you're not sure where, a summer abroad in just any ole country won't be nearly as impressive to employers as work experience is. For instance, if you want to work in the foreign office of a large, domestic law firm—they all do have very glamorous-sounding foreign offices—you're far better off getting summer experience that will get your foot in the door at that firm, BV. At the risk of pointing out the obvious, employers are far more concerned with your job skills and dedication to working than they are to hands-on proof that you like to travel (which you can easily prove with a spring break in England). Those foreign office plums are typically either staffed with people from those countries or with associates with a few domestic years under their belts, for whom a foreign assignment is something of a reward.

At this point, BV, you may wonder why it is that any loving, caring law schools hawk international programs so fiercely—and so persuasively. The bottom line, BV, is—the bottom line. International programs are money-makers for schools, and very desirable carrots to dangle in front of the professors who get to teach them. While that's not a particularly benevolent motive, it's perfectly understandable. Unlike the Job Goddess, not everybody is slavishly devoted to what's best for your career, BV.

So, what should you do? "Isn't there some way to pro-
mote my career **and** go to Greece?" you're silently asking
the Job Goddess. Well, yes. There is a happy compro-
mise, and all it takes is a bit of planning. Do your summer program, get your tan—oops, sorry—do your
studying—and spend the other half of your summer
getting job experience of the type the Job Goddess
described earlier. A six-week summer program still
leaves you with six weeks stateside, and even if you need
to make money with that time (although if you've got
the jack to go abroad, money may not be an issue), you
can always work part-time for six weeks and get volunteer experience part-time. Or you could put in a full
week getting your legal tootsies wet, and waiter on weekends for dough. That way you've got something interesting on your resume and something worthwhile in your
head—and if that isn't a pleasant *pot de creme*, the Job
Goddess doesn't know what is.

Bon voyage, BV!

ETERNALLY YOURS,

The Job Goddess

Plotting

Where to Go to School?
Where to Work?

How Employable Will I Be if I Go to "Not-Harvard"?

Dear Job Goddess,

I am contemplating law school and have been accepted, thus far, to the Massachusetts School of Law. Economically and schedulewise it makes sense. My question is, as far as future employment is concerned, does it matter what law school you went to?

KJ, Massachusetts

Dear KJ,

Of course, KJ, it never *hurts* to go to Harvard. The extent to which it hurts *not* to go to Harvard? That depends—but the Job Goddess assures you that ultimately, whatever your dream job is, you can get it regardless of where you decide to go to law school. And why is that? As Teresa DeAndrado, former Career Services Director at Washington University School of Law, says, "People hire people, not law schools."

Having said that, *does* it make a difference where you go to school? Well, yes, at least in the short term—in the sense that your school can make it *easier* to *break into* your dream job. There's no question that if you attend one of the law schools that are considered distinguished—and let's face it, KJ, you either know them, or you know where to find them, since they include Harvard, Yale, Michigan, and NYU (and a handful of others whose feathers the Job Goddess has just ruffled by not mentioning them in the same breath)—*and* you don't sit on your brains for three years, your quest *for your very first job* (and *only* your first job) is going to be easier simply because potential employers will be impressed with the name on your diploma (and here I refer to the name of your *school,* not your own name, KJ). Future jobs are a different story, but for that first one, yes, a Yale diploma will certainly grease the wheels to get you in the door. But there is so much more to this story, KJ!

The sources with whom the Job Goddess conferred on your question—and for obvious reasons of professional security, they chose to remain nameless—agreed that outside of those distinguished schools, school "rankings," regardless of the source, are not very meaningful. Instead, there are three factors to consider: where you want to live, what you want to do, and how well you do in law school (which of course is a great big question mark for you right now).

First, location. While the prospect of "seeing another part of the country" lures many an unsuspecting law student to school thousands of miles from where they intend to settle, that's not the best career move. You're far better off being near where you want to settle down, since your opportunities to take part in local activities, to see and be seen in either paid or volunteer positions, will smooth your transition into practicing law. Furthermore, employers tend to view students from local law schools more kindly than a school that is technically "better" but further away, simply by dint of familiarity. What if you don't know where you want to live? Well, the Job Goddess hears you, and responds with the obvious insight that if that's the case, then location isn't a factor you can use in your favor.

Second, you've got to consider what it is that you want to do. It may well be that you want to open your own practice, or you just want a law degree as a kind of bonus credential for present or future employers, since they don't respond so favorably to a set of ginsu knives. If that's the case, it doesn't much matter where you go to school; the important thing for you to do is to get your diploma. For instance, the Job Goddess knows of some detectives who went to law school at night while they kept their day jobs, and as soon as they graduated, they hung out a shingle doing criminal defense work. With that kind of background, who's going to care where they went to school, right?

But the way you phrased your letter, KJ, suggests that's not you—you want to know who's going to hire you. If you have a well-defined specialty you want to pursue, it's worth checking with lawyers who practice that specialty to see if there's a particular school, among your choices, that makes more sense to attend. For instance, in New England, Franklin Pierce in Concord, New Hampshire, is very well known for its Intellectual Property program. And on the West Coast, the University of Oregon births many an environmental lawyer from its highly-regarded Environmental Law program. If you want a particular specialty and go to a school known for that specialty, finding that first job will clearly be easier for you.

With employability being a significant concern for you, the Job Goddess would recommend calling the career services director at any law school you're considering, and ask specific questions about employment. What do most people from the school wind up doing? What's the route most of them use to find their first job? Does the school have a mentoring program, or otherwise helpful alumni? You will think of many other questions as well, but the Job Goddess cautions you that placement rates are not terribly helpful, because they look at employment six months after graduation. A number of factors can delay law school graduates from finding a first job—like, oh, say, flunking the bar—but within a year after graduation, virtually everybody is employed. And that's why numbers aren't helpful.

Other than going straight to the source and talking with career services at your potential law schools, you can look through a directory of lawyers in the city where you want to practice (any law library will have such a directory), and check to see where they went to law school. As a rule of thumb, lawyers will view graduates of their alma mater with favor. (One career services director told the Job Goddess about the partner at a prestigious law firm who *always* made job offers to any law student who attended the partner's school and could sing the school's fight song. And since the song featured some hearty "oom-pah-pah's," the humiliation factor was significant.)

Finally, the ease with which you'll nail that first job depends on your law school grades. Notice that the Job Goddess said *ease,* not *ability*—because she must constantly reiterate that your grades in law school do not define your career! But the fact is, if you do extremely well in law school, *especially* in your first year, virtually any employer will welcome you *regardless* of which law school you attend (assuming, as the Job Goddess does, that you do not have the personality of a garden slug). Unfortunately, grades as a career determinant are overemphasized by virtually everyone, and the Job Goddess cautions you *against* listening to much of the well-meaning but misguided advice you will receive from others, who will tell you there's no point in attending law school if you're not in the top 10% of your class. How, the Job Goddess wonders, is it possible to *know* that *before you go?* Sigh. If you are not at the top of your class, KJ, you will simply speed up the necessity of learning and employing the job search skills that will serve you well for the rest of your life. *That's all.*

Did you notice a theme running through this column, KJ? The Job Goddess's emphasis on your law school's impact on your *first* job? Her reason for that is that she knows something you will soon discover—it really ultimately doesn't matter *where* you go to school.

Within a couple of years of graduation, you aren't your school, or your grades. You're *you*, and whatever you make of your career. So *ultimately*, from a whole life perspective, does your choice of school impact your future employment?

In a word—no. Isn't that reassuring?

ETERNALLY YOURS,

The Job Goddess

If I Start My Career in New York, Will I Be Able to Cash in on the Cachet of the City?

Dear Job Goddess,

I am a second-year law student in New York City. My problem is that I am seriously considering moving back to California after I graduate. My question is, how will this move affect my career? Should I try to work for a couple of years at a "big NYC law firm" before moving out to the West Coast? Or should I move out there from the start? Or should I choose the firm that will provide me with the best training regardless of location? I ask this because it seems like there is a degree of respect granted to people with experience at a big NYC firm that doesn't go along with other kinds of experience.

Very curious,

EK, NY

Dear EK,

So, the prospect of easy access to the world's best bagels, and being able to find the Sunday *New York Times* as early as Thursday, aren't enough by themselves to keep you in New York? All right, EK, let's look at whether kicking off your career in New York will leave a permanent luster on your resume.

The answer depends greatly on what kind of career you see yourself having *after* you escape from New York. After all, as Joan King, Director of the Career Center at Brooklyn Law School, advises, "One of the biggest selling points of major law firms is that having them on your resume gives you some flexibility later on." Whether that flexibility encompasses your own dream job depends on what that dream *is*, EK. Joan King explains, for instance, that if you want to be a U.S. Attorney (which, as you may know, is one of the plummiest legal jobs in existence), large firm experience is very valuable. Similarly, judges frequently hire judicial clerks out of huge firms.

What if you want a private employer, presumably at a small to medium-sized firm? Joan King suggests that you look through Martindale-Hubbell for the place where you want to live, and see if the attorneys in the community tend to have big firm experience in their backgrounds. She explains, "In some communities, the attorneys really think it's great if you've got a mega-firm in your background. And some kinds of employers love for their associates to have huge firm experience. They know that you'll have meticulous, in-depth research skills, and they also know that with the long hours a large firm demands in your recent past, you'll want the quality of life (and accept the pay cut) that a smaller employer offers. In other communities, mentioning that you're from a large firm will scare employers away." Another way of skinning the same cat is to check with your alumni relations office at school and find alumni who are working in the community. Call or write to them, and ask them the same question you've asked the Job Goddess: "I intend to live and practice there, and I'm wondering about the value of getting New York experience first, at a large firm. Based on what you know about the legal community there, what do you think?"

You may have noticed, EK, that the Job Goddess has been focusing primarily on the fact that you're thinking of starting your career at a large firm, not specifically a large firm in **New York**. Why is that? Because the benefits of large firm experience apply to *any* large, well-known law firm, anywhere in America. There isn't a particular magic to run-of-the-mill New York experience in and of itself—unless, of course, you want to stay in New York. Instead, Joan King advises that "It's much more important to be plugged into the community where you really want to be, and let them know that that's what you really want." In the time you'd spend getting your feet wet in New York, you'd be making contacts in your dream town—and those contacts translate into business, which is valuable to *any* private employer. So it may be a matter of pride for you that you can locate take-out Ethiopian food in Manhattan at three a.m., but that's unlikely to play well with a law firm in Peoria.

By the way, EK, the Job Goddess is very proud of you. It's difficult to look past the glamour—and paychecks—of New York mega-firms, and consider those jobs as they relate to pursuing the life you love. The Job Goddess applauds you for doing so.

ETERNALLY YOURS,

The Job Goddess

A Law Degree: Can You Get It Now, Use It Later?

I am curious: What would it do to my later legal career to take a non-legal job after law school? I am considering a position as a financial consultant, and I am also considering pursuing my boyhood dream of being a police officer. What do you advise?

SC, New York

Dear SC,

You're not alone in wanting to hold your law degree in a state of suspended animation while you pursue something else, SC, so let's talk about how you go about accomplishing that.

As a rule of thumb, "The closer your immediate dream job is to a practice area or legal topic, the easier it is to go back," according to Mary Birmingham, Dean of Career Services at the University of Arizona Law School. So if you, for instance, pursue your financial consulting option, you'd expect a fairly smooth transition to practicing corporate law. On the other hand, if you opted to travel the world as a lion tamer, you'd encounter predictable difficulty selling a law firm on your professional assets (although expertise with a whip can be an advantage in so many adversarial situations, don't you agree?).

Take into account, SC, that it would be up to *you* at the end of your hiatus from law to come up with *exactly* what it is you bring to the law firm table as a result of your experience, whether you spend that time as a

21

financial consultant, software designer, spy, whatever. Mary Birmingham herself spent the first few years after law school working for a labor union, handling arbitrations and mediations. When she decided to try practicing law after all, she successfully sold herself to litigation firms as someone who knew how to present a position and represent clients. She points out that if your other experience has put you in a position to bring in clients—making you the golden goose of law in the form of a rainmaker—that is a huge plus. So if you try financial consulting, keep that Rolodex up-to-date and that Christmas card list humming.

At this point you may be wondering, "Why, Job Goddess, have you glossed over the police officer option?" Because the Job Goddess is sensitive to the idea of building up to a climax, that's why. And what makes the police officer option the climax here? Because you said so yourself, SC—*it's your dream,* and those are magic words to the Job Goddess. Although you didn't ask, you'll find that your law degree is a real asset as a police officer. As Mary Birmingham points out, "Although it's unusual for a police officer to have a law degree, it will make it much easier for you to advance through the ranks."

When it comes to making the trip back to practicing law . . . well, nothing is impossible. It's actually a lot easier to do things in a different order than you propose, namely, police officer → law student → lawyer, rather than your idea of law student → police officer → lawyer. As Peggy McCartney, Assistant Career Services Director at Washington University School of Law in St. Louis (and herself a former prosecutor) says, "A police background for lawyers is great." The flip-flop you're proposing? Peggy McCartney says, "Why not combine your two interests, and consider the FBI, where having a law degree is a real plus, and field officers are really glorified police officers. Or try the Drug Enforcement Agency, or even the prosecutor's office. Any one of those may fulfill your desire to be a white knight." She goes on to say that the problem with being a police officer now and a lawyer later on is that "Police technology is not like getting technical skills as a lawyer. It's not impossible to make the transition, but the distance between your law degree and practicing law creates problems." In other words, SC, it's not impossible to do *exactly* what you asked the Job Goddess . . . but why bother, when you can do something *right now* that might fulfill everything you want? Why have your law degree hanging over your head like the sword of Damocles (look it up), making you feel guiltier and guiltier as the years go by? And if you think and think and think about it and it's being a police officer you really want, then resolve yourself to being an extraordinarily well-educated cop. It's your life, and your dream, SC—and if it ultimately doesn't mean flexing that law degree eight hours a day, there's no crime in that.

ETERNALLY YOURS,

The Job Goddess

Pulling Rabbits Out of Hats

Getting What You've Convinced Yourself You're Not Qualified to Get

How Do I Get My Own Law Firm Without Starting My Own Law Firm?

DEAR JOB GODDESS,

I am currently clerking at a large personal injury firm in Washington, D.C. I want to be a trial lawyer, but if I start my career here, I will just be shuffling hundreds of worker's comp files. I don't really want to hang out my own shingle. Instead, I've been thinking that I would like to find a job with a senior lawyer who wants to slowly wind down his or her practice, and wants to handle big cases but is looking for a 'mentee' to try the smaller cases. What do you think is the best way to accomplish this seemingly impossible task? I feel like I am trying to locate a needle in a haystack.

DH, Maryland

DEAR DH,

Impossible? Needles? Haystacks? Why, this is exactly the kind of quagmire in which the Job Goddess loves to wallow. Your goal is actually very much easier to attain than you think, DH. And on top of that, the Job Goddess applauds you for seeking a job which is likely to bring you a great deal of happiness.

There are several methods for finding the retiring lawyers you seek. There are two direct routes which are likely to bear fruit most quickly. One is to go to local bar association meetings, make a point of introducing yourself to people, and tell everyone whose ear you can bend exactly what it is that you want. Make a special effort to meet the head of the litigation section of your local bar, since it's trial work that you want to do.

Along the same lines, go to the local courthouse whenever you can, taking a morning or afternoon off work, if need be. Introduce yourself to the court clerk, bailiffs, judges, and tell them what you're looking for. After all, they're going to know every trial attorney, and will certainly be able to identify the ones who are golf course bound. On top of that, they'll be a great source for weeding out the good eggs from the bad ones, since they've seen local trial lawyers operate first hand!

With either of these direct methods, DH, be sure that you impress every person you meet, even though they will not be your ultimate employer. Smile. Seem enthusiastic. Stress your willingness to work hard in return for soaking up knowledge from an experienced lawyer. Your first impression on the people you meet will have a dramatic effect on their willingness to help you—and what they'll tell the senior lawyers they know!

A somewhat less direct route, but one not to be overlooked, is to go to the career services office at your law school, talk to the director, and explain your goal. Most law students do not appreciate what a gold mine of information their career services directors really are— they do so much more than organize on-campus interviews! So it may be that you need go no further than your own law school. Or your own law firm, for that matter—if you don't mind the people you work with knowing that you're looking elsewhere, tell your colleagues about your goal. The benefit here is that because the lawyers at your firm are familiar with your work and know what it's like to work with you, they'll tend to think of people for whom you'd be a good work *and* personality fit.

If you insist on taking an initial step that doesn't involve talking with people, there are a couple of fertile resources you can use. One is to let your fingers do the walking—check the Yellow Pages! Look up the names of sole practitioners who are litigators (the Yellow Pages will mention their specialties), and then look them up in Martindale-Hubbell. (You can find Mar-Hub on-line, at http://lawyers.martindale.com/marhub). Look at their graduation dates, and when you find ones that are about 30 years ago, you've got a potential target audience for your letters. The Job Goddess would tell you what to say in those letters, DH, except that this simple column would become 50 pages long. Instead, she encourages you to borrow—or, dare she suggest it, *buy*—a copy of her runaway bestseller, *Guerrilla Tactics for Getting the Legal Job of Your Dreams*, and read the chapter entitled "Correspondence—Making Your Letters Sing."

You might also consider getting on-line. You can go to a chat room or enroll in a LISTSERV for your state and/or local bar association; more and more state bar associations have such facilities, and the Job Goddess knows of enterprising students who have gone to these chat rooms and LISTSERVs, waited for an opportune moment, and pitched their services to the members— with glorious results. To find out the web addresses for these resources, call the relevant bar association.

You may even want to consider doing a reverse job ad. That is, run an ad looking for a practice. What you'll want to do is to put an ad in the classifieds section of a publication that goes to your target audience, like your local or state bar journal or even a newspaper. In your ad, don't just state what you're looking for; emphasize your willingness and desire to work hard.

No matter which route you choose, DH, remember the nature of your quest. When a sole practitioner hires someone on, the relationship resembles a marriage more than a traditional partner-associate connection. The personal relationship you develop is of paramount importance. So be sure to look for someone who is on your wavelength, and don't be discouraged if you and any one lawyer don't "click"—if you do as the Job Goddess advises, there will be plenty of fish in your ocean.

E T E R N A L L Y   Y O U R S ,

The Job Goddess

How Can I Get an In-House Counsel Job Straight Out of Law School?

DEAR JOB GODDESS,

I am halfway through law school and am just beginning to seriously look for a job. I have always wanted to work in a corporation's legal department, but it seems like they always want someone with several years of experience in practice. Is there any way around this?

KS, Kentucky

DEAR KS,

The Job Goddess gets many letters like yours, KS, basically asking the same question: "Is it possible to get to Heaven without dying first?" In this instance, the Job Goddess is happy to tell you that the answer is yes.

Let's talk for a moment about the nature of the problem you face, KS. And in doing so let's say that you run the MiB Clothing Company, which specializes in exactly one style of black suit. You need to have some lawyers in-house. Who are you going to choose? Somebody who has some experience in legal practice, who may be able to foresee and quickly handle potential legal problems? Or somebody with a freshly-minted law school diploma, all enthusiasm but lacking hands-on knowledge? Ah, you see the difficulty companies face, and why it is that they typically require a few years worth of "real law" under your belt before they'll hire you. But having said that, not *every* company fits that mold, and the Job Goddess being the Job Goddess, she can't let you down. Let's see how to overcome that little matter of practical experience.

There are two basic ways to skin the in-house counsel cat. One is to look for companies that are sufficiently large that they can afford to have new lawyers cut their teeth there. Some even have internship programs, the corporate equivalent of a summer associateship. Your career services office will have resources that tell you who these companies are. As an alternative, you can do a little footwork of your own and call the human resources departments at any large corporations that interest you, and ask them directly if their legal department has such a program. Needless to say, companies that have internship programs will typically hire new full-time lawyers from those programs, and presumably when their interns don't work out, they will hire new graduates, as well.

Aside from internship programs, there *are* a few large companies that routinely hire new law school graduates for their in-house counsel departments. One that comes to the Job Goddess's mind is Procter & Gamble, which has a law department that rivals the size of many large firms, including a number of new law school graduates. (Coincidentally, P&G is supposed to be a wonderful place to work; so wonderful, in fact, that it appears in the Job Goddess's book, *America's Greatest Places to Work With a Law Degree*. If you're curious about why it's so great, turn to Appendix A.)

Another option is to go to the other end of the scale, to very small companies. As Mary Birmingham, Career Services Director at the University of Arizona School of Law, points out, "Look for small companies that can't afford someone with huge experience!" She recounts a couple of stories about recent law school graduates who did exactly that. One of them went to a new technology company that wanted a law school graduate who was interested in helping to get the business off the ground. The other went to a construction company that needed someone to be able to interpret and negotiate contracts, as well as help out on the business end. As she says, "Think about what it takes to run a business! Every business needs somebody to negotiate contracts, watch out for potential liabilities, be aware of insurance matters. As a small business person, a lawyer is your right hand."

Mary Birmingham also points out, KS, that you may want to look at corporations as more than a source of in-house counsel jobs. The Job Goddess knows of many companies that hire law school graduates not as lawyers, but in all sorts of other interesting capacities. For instance, many multinational companies hire law school graduates as contract negotiators. You aren't technically a 'lawyer,' but on the plus side, you certainly get to use your legal knowledge doing interesting work, and you frequently get to travel to all kinds of exotic places. And when it comes to opportunities to advance, as Mary Birmingham explains, "You can make **much** more money moving up the business side than the legal side of a corporation. Companies have only one general counsel, but there are **many** steps up the ladder on the business side that will outstrip others in the legal department." For information on these kinds of opportunities, Bill Barrett, Jr., Career Services Director at the Wake Forest University School of Law, has an ingenious idea. He suggests that you visit the undergrad or MBA school affiliated with your law school (or your own undergrad alma mater), talk to the career services people *there*, and find out which corporations come on campus to interview. He says that those same companies may be ones who are interested in J.D.s for the business track, as well.

In short, KS, there are many incredible opportunities open to you, doing exactly what you want to do: namely, starting off in a corporate environment. Now that you know what they are, the Job Goddess encourages you to put your energy into finding—and pursuing—those opportunities!

ETERNALLY YOURS,

The Job Goddess

"Show Me the Money!"–Turning a Computer Background and a Law Degree Into Big Bucks

Dear Job Goddess,

I am a third-year law student. Law will be my second career. Before law school, I was heavily involved in microcomputers. I started a $3 million business, consulted, and am now somewhat of an Internet guru. My question is this: What kind of position should I be seeking where the employer will say, "Wow, we really need this guy, let's give him lots of money." Unfortunately, since I'm still in school, I don't have much legal experience.

Thank you in advance, oh goddess of jobs.

TD, USA

Dear TD,

The Job Goddess applauds bluntness like yours, TD. No nattering on about job satisfaction, just a simple, heartfelt plea: "Show me the money!" In fact, as Orson Welles pointed out in the film *Citizen Kane*, it's not difficult to make a lot of money, if money is all you want. Let's see how you, TD, can turn a bit of computer knowledge and a law degree into a shower of doubloons and pieces of eight.

As Deidre Washington, Assistant Dean and Director of Career Services at St. Thomas University Law School, points out, "You're in a better position than most law students, with a strong background in computers." A career she recommends to you is director of automation for a law library. Why? "All law libraries are anxious about entering the 21st century, and so they are looking for people who can help them make the leap to computerization." Obviously this isn't the job for everyone— you do need a strong computer background. But on the plus side, you don't need a technical undergrad degree, and—here's the key—these kinds of positions can have a starting salary around a hundred thousand smackers.

You've got other options as well, of course. One that Deidre Washington recommends is going back to all of those people you worked with while climbing the ranks to the position of grand poobah in your pre-law school career, letting them know that you've now added a law degree to your credential quiver, and seeing what develops.

Now because the Job Goddess is ultimately concerned with your welfare, she can't leave you like this, TD. Even though you sloughed off any mention of career satisfaction, the Job Goddess encourages you to think at least a little bit about exactly what kind of work-related activities will make you happy. After all, if you can't get past the stereotype of nerds and wizened old Yoda-like librarians hissing "sshhh!," a library position of any kind may not be your cup of tea, regardless of how much it pays (and how far your perception may be from the truth). So before you leap at any high-paying job, talk to people who've already taken the plunge into it and see if what they do with their time is something you'd enjoy. Then, TD, you've got the best of all possible worlds—a job you look forward to performing, and a platinum American Express card.

ETERNALLY YOURS,

The Job Goddess

Overcoming the "Why-Should-We-Hire-You-You've-Got-No-Experience" Problem

DEAR JOB GODDESS,

I am a recent law school graduate, unemployed right now but very hopeful. I did some work for a local attorney drafting a brief on a high-profile criminal case. He suggested that I interview with someone he knows at the county attorney's office. The job is for prosecuting misdemeanors and backing up a child support attorney. I know that they want litigation and criminal experience. What should I say when they ask me why I'm the one they should hire? I thought about highlighting my recent work drafting that brief, and adding that I'm a quick study and would work hard at getting up to speed as fast as I could. What do you think, Job Goddess?

PA, Nebraska

Dear PA,

Why, you have a bit of the Goddess in you! Faced with a problem many law students encounter—a lack of experience—you have shown your instincts to be excellent. Let's talk about why this is so, and the steps that *anybody* in your slippers could take to turn the ruins of their resume into a temple.

First of all, you've clearly researched what your prospective employer *wants*. The Job Goddess knows this sounds basic, but you'd be astounded how many law students walk into interviews with a knowledge of the employer that can be summed up by the word, "duh." Statistics show that 19 out of 20 interviewees walk in absolutely cold! Why is doing even the most rudimentary research so very important? Because once you *know* what an employer wants, you can both fashion your own background to fit those desires, do brush-up work *right now* to add luster to your credentials, and show what you're willing to do *in the future* to meet the employer's needs. The wonderful little secret in finding your dream job is this: it just doesn't matter what you've done *until* now. It matters what you do and say, *starting now.*

In terms of molding what you've done to suit the employer's needs, first of all be sure to comb your background for transferable skills. If the job you want entails a lot of contact with children, and you were once a camp counselor, highlight that. If it entails a lot of research, stress that semester you spent researching Professor Shamalama's Law Review article. You get the point. Apart from exploiting what you *do* have to bring to the table, if you just don't have much experience in what they do, don't be afraid to explode your own land mine by admitting it—*in a confident way.* As Sue Kirkland, Career Services Director at the University of Nebraska College of Law, says, "Be honest that you're lacking experience, but don't just say, 'I know I don't have the credentials you want . . . .' Say something like, 'I may not have a whole lot of experience, but I *do* have this experience working for yah-de-yah on this case, I've done all of these other things that the Job Goddess is going to explain in the next two paragraphs, and apart from that, I'm willing to do whatever is necessary to get up to speed.'"

Here are those 'other things,' PA. What you've got to do right now is to back up your claim that you'll do whatever you need to do to hit the ground running! Sue Kirkland advises that you "Shake the trees to find people who'll help you learn what you need to know, *fast*. Go to your career services office and see who from your school does the kind of work you're looking for, or ask any other contacts, at school or in the community, that you might have." Talk to those people, explain the situation, and find out from them what's important for you to know about the job you want, as well as any other steps you should take. You never know how helpful people will be, but the Job Goddess assures you that people will genuinely surprise you with what they're willing to give! As Sue Kirkland recounts, "I had a student who came to me with a similar request. As it turns out, I knew a graduate who worked at the county attorney's office. I called that graduate and asked if this student could follow him around for a day, to get familiar with the work the student would be doing if he got a job there. That one day worked miracles for that student!"

Another thing you can do is to take continuing legal education seminars that people in your dream position would take. Even if you don't have time to take any seminars before your interview, you can make a few calls today to your local bar association to see what's going to be offered by way of CLEs, and when. And make sure you mention the steps you've taken when you interview! You'll say something like, "I called the local bar to find out when CLEs would be offered, and I'll be taking one next week. Also, I spent a day following Booboo Trizwitz, from your office, around."

What's really going on here, PA? It's something you have perhaps already divined. ***Enthusiasm*** is a cure-all for virtually any credential ailment. In a sea of apathy, a job applicant who goes to the kind of effort the Job Goddess has outlined for you will stand out like a beacon. And the Job Goddess trusts that you will do exactly that.

E T E R N A L L Y   Y O U R S ,

The Job Goddess

Hopping Onto the Intellectual Property Bandwagon Without a Technical Undergrad Degree

Dear Job Goddess,

I'm a second-year law student who is very much interested in pursuing a career as an intellectual property attorney, along either prosecution or defense lines. My problem, in a nutshell, is this: no technical degree. I'm not a technical illiterate; I've been using computers regularly for more than 10 years. But I've never set foot in a computer class, and my bachelor's degree is about as nontechnical as they come.

The result of this common but apparently crippling malady is that I'm excluded from taking the Patent Bar exam—an exclusion which is often ending my job search at IP law firms before it even begins.

*Is there any way to effectively combat this situation without returning to school for yet **another** two years after law school to earn a technical degree I neither want nor, God-willing, that I need?*

JC, Oregon

Dear Job Goddess,

Help me! I'm a second-year in law school, and I would like to work in intellectual property. However, all of my previous experience is in criminal prosecution. Can you offer any advice on job search and interview (God-willing!) strategies?

CL, Los Angeles

Dear JC and CL,

Crippling malady, not having a technical undergrad degree? Pshaw! Certainly you know the Job Goddess well enough to know that there's no such thing as a crippling malady when it comes to finding your dream job. Annoying head colds, maybe, but certainly nothing worse than **that**.

What you want to get into, without perhaps realizing it, is what's known as "soft intellectual property." By this the Job Goddess doesn't mean "easy" or that **you** have to be soft, but rather it's an area of intellectual property that does **not** require a technical undergraduate degree. Better yet, as Susan Richey, Career Services Director at Franklin Pierce Law Center points out, "**Tons** of people do it!"

To differentiate soft intellectual property from, the Job Goddess supposes, **hard** intellectual property, you are correct, JC, in pointing out that hard intellectual property requires a technical undergrad and passing the patent bar. Soft intellectual property, by contrast, involves "virtually any kind of intangible property," according to Susan Richey. So, for instance, telecommunications law, and the wildly-popular Internet subset of that, would be considered soft intellectual property. As would trademarks and copyrights, and sometimes even sports and entertainment law, although sports and entertainment tend to focus more on contract issues.

The Job Goddess suspects that having read that list of possibilities, you are champing at the bit with the question, "So, how do you break into these ultra-glamorous specialties?" In much the same way you'd break into any *other* specialty, namely: start working toward your goal *right now*. In school, seek out externships during the summer or even during winter break. Since many soft intellectual property specialties involve government agencies and other public interest-oriented organizations, Susan Richey suggests that you sit down with a book like *The Public Interest Law Guide* that Harvard Law School puts out (your career services office probably has it) and get a feel for what's out there. The Job Goddess knows that you cringe at this concept, but seriously consider volunteering in order to get experience. Work evenings at a restaurant, tutor, or do whatever you will in order to pay your bills, but when you want to enter fields as glamorous as these, any relevant experience gives you a tremendous advantage, both as a credential and as an opportunity to meet people who can help usher you into the field.

Another option to consider in overcoming the lack of technical background is getting a joint degree (the Job Goddess realizes that this is not particularly attractive to you, JC). Franklin Pierce, for instance, offers a Masters in Intellectual Property, in a tranquil New England setting to boot. The Job Goddess emphasizes that you *can* break in *without* additional education, but having such a degree is obviously another arrow in your professional quiver.

The Job Goddess cautions you that while her up-to-the-minute advice reflects the world as it exists today, you will encounter many people who will try and discourage you, insisting that you need a technical background in order to get into intellectual property. As Susan Richey points out, "Traditionally, intellectual property firms did require a technical degree. But the reality today is that they don't hire people just to do patents. They hire people to do trademarks and copyrights as well, and those don't require a technical degree."

So you have your marching orders, JC and CL. Find a subspecialty you like, and hunt down a part-time job or externship (paid or not). And as the Job Goddess always counsels, become familiar with every publication in your chosen field, read about people and issues, and contact people you read about and authors whose articles you like, praising their work and asking their advice. Get on mailing lists in your dream specialty and go to every seminar and presentation you can find. In other words, pretend you're already doing what it is you dream of doing. And soon, very soon, you really *will* be starting your dream career—technical degree or not.

ETERNALLY YOURS,

The Job Goddess

The Emerald City

Getting Into Large Firms

Where Are the Big Bucks in the Big Apple?

Dear Job Goddess,

 Which firm pays the most in New York City?

HR, New York

Dear HR,

It may surprise you to learn that this is ***almost*** the most frequently asked question the Job Goddess receives, HR. (To sate your curiosity, the ***most*** frequently-asked question comes from foreign law students asking, 'How do I get a job in the United States?' which the Job Goddess supposes she really ought to answer. But not right now.)

Of course, the question of phattest cash doesn't always involve New York, but it is always a large U.S. city, and ***occasionally*** the Job Goddess's correspondents even name firms: "Does Fleece & Flounder pay more than Snap, Crackle, and Popp?"

Fortunately, the Job Goddess can answer the question of 'who pays the most' very simply: Every large firm in the same city ultimately pays the same.

"What?" the Job Goddess hears you protest. "That's not what *I* read!" Perhaps not, but having spoken with many large-firm lawyers in many cities—off the record, of course—the Job Goddess can assure you that this is true, for one simple reason: they have to. Why? Because they are all competing for the same minuscule sterlingly-paper-credentialled law student gene pool. That's why, when one major firm ups the ante, its neighbors immediately follow suit.

Now it may be that a wily firm will try and lure you with talk of hefty bonuses, HR, but the Job Goddess cautions you to eye those bonuses with great suspicion. The Job Goddess has known of more than one firm that offers bonuses that sound lavish, but are, in practice, unattainable.

Instead, if you are the Scarlett O'Hara of law students and find yourself with many avid large-firm suitors, make your choice on the basis of non-monetary issues: the work you'll do, and perhaps even more importantly, the people you'll do it *for* and *with*.

And anyway, HR, if it's really big bucks you're after—you know that no law firm pays the most coming out of the starting gate. McKinsey, the huge and prestigious consulting firm, does. So if it's phenomenal opening buckage that flips your switch, and you've got amazing credentials, then consider being a management consultant *instead* of a large firm associate.

The Job Goddess hopes that she doesn't sound corny by hoping that you choose the job that makes you the happiest. And of course, if that happy job also means big bucks, the Job Goddess trusts that next time she is in New York City, you'll give her a ride in your new Porsche.

E T E R N A L L Y   Y O U R S ,

The Job Goddess

⟨⟩⟨⟩⟨⟩

I Want a Large Firm, But I Don't Have the Grades. Can I Paralegal My Way In?

DEAR JOB GODDESS,

I'm dying to work at a big firm here in Florida. However, I have a 2.0 average, so I know there's no way they are going to let me in the usual way. They are willing to interview me as a paralegal. Is that a good way to break in, and then move over to being an associate?

AT, Fort Lauderdale

DEAR AT,

As you know, the Job Goddess never says "No." However, in your case, AT, there are other ways to break into this particular heavenly law firm—means that are more interesting, more fun, and—ahem—more likely.

The idea of breaking into large firms via the paralegal route is, alas, an outdated one. It's true that 20 years ago, it was possible to do this; you may find partners at large firms who actually got their start this way. However, nowadays you're about as likely to spot Elvis at a Seven-Eleven as you are to make the move from paralegal to associate at a large firm.

Why is that? For the answer to this question, the Job Goddess turned to the wonderful Anne Stark Walker, Career Services Director at the University of Denver College of Law, who in a prior life was hiring partner at a very large law firm. She says that, "Once you are iden-tified in a particular role in a law firm, it's **very** hard to change people's minds. It's not fair, but that's the way it is." Is it **impossible**? Well, no, any more than it's impos-sible that you'd spot Elvis at the Seven-Eleven. But it's very difficult. As Anne Walker says, "You'd have to show stupendous initiative, and you'd need to make an extra-ordinary effort to make yourself valuable. Even then, law firms are suspicious of paralegals with higher ambitions."

The Job Goddess knows of one extraordinary young man who did, in fact, break the paralegal mold, but when you hear this story, AT, you'll see what it takes to step into an associate position by the means you suggest. This particular young man got his foot in the door at his dream law firm with the only job they offered him—a third shift proofreader, working in the basement. ("Ugh," the Job Goddess can hear you saying to yourself. Well, hold on. It gets much, much better!) Proofreading the firm's documents from midnight to 8 a.m. every day, this guy got a better idea than any other single person exactly what was "hot" there. The telecommunications department was putting out volumes of material, and this young man decided that department was going to be his entré to the firm. He familiarized himself with all kinds of telecommunications law publications, and found that there was going to be a national telecommunications law conference in town shortly. He volunteered to help out, and wound up summarizing all of the presenta-tions and writing up the minutes. The conference put out a newsletter featuring everything he'd written, put his name on the materials, and sent the newsletter to every telecommunications lawyer in the country. The newsletter wound up on the desk of the partner in charge of the telecommunications department at this guy's firm—six stories above him! The partner was impressed with the newsletter, looked for the name of the person who wrote it, and when he saw it, he buzzed his secretary and said: "Why does this name ring a bell?" She responded, "It's the kid in the basement." He said, "He doesn't belong in the basement. Get him up here!" When the partner confronted the young guy and asked him if the newsletter was his work, the guy 'fessed up, and the partner said, "Why did you do this?" He said he had read everything the partner's department was putting out and found it fascinating, and wanted to develop an expertise in it. The partner, duly impressed, made him an associate—the only new associate in this very hot field at the firm!

So, certainly, AT, lightning strikes occasionally. But what's the easier way to accomplish your dream? As Anne Walker advises, "You're so much better off if you go to a smaller firm or even get into an office sharing situation with another lawyer acting as a mentor. Develop your own client base, develop expertise in a niche area—and two or three years from now, go back to that firm. At that point, they won't look at your grades, because your track record will trump your grades. You'll have shown them what you can do, which is so much more important than your grades ever could be."

In short, AT, the best way for you to get into your dream firm is to start somewhere else first, and move over as a full-fledged lawyer. If you want, look at those first two years as an apprenticeship, so that you won't feel you're compromising your dreams—because you're not. You're just taking a different, more creative, route to making them come true.

ETERNALLY YOURS,

The Job Goddess

I'm a Big Fish in a Puddle—At the Top of My Class at a Poorly-Ranked Law School. If I Want a Big Firm, Should I Transfer?

Dear Job Goddess,

I am currently a first-year law student. My goal is to land a job with a large law firm. I currently attend a fourth-tier (according to U.S. News) school and rank first in my class. My question is, should I transfer to a first-tier school, or stay where I am?

JH, Michigan

Dear JH,

The Job Goddess would like to congratulate you, JH, on sending her the thorniest question she has ever received. She has consulted with a variety of law school administrators, both from highly-ranked as well as—well—not-so-highly-ranked schools, as well as recruiting coordinators at large law firms, to fashion an answer for you. For fairly predictable reasons, she's not going to quote any of them by name, but she is certain that the advice she learned is spot-on, and it boils down to this: You probably don't have to transfer if you don't want to, and if you *do*, there are a few issues for you to consider.

First of all, consider where it is, geographically, that you want to wind up. Once you've figured that out, take a look at the Martindale Hubbell listing of lawyers in the large firms in town (you can find MarHub at your career services office, or on-line at http://lawyers. martindale.com/marhub). Look at where the junior-ish associates went to law school, the ones hired in the last five years or so. If your school has a particularly harsh reputation—which is extremely unlikely—you may find that they just don't hire from your school. The Job Goddess has known large firms to say to students from particularly struggling law schools, "We'd hire you but we don't want lawyers with a diploma from your school on our walls." Ouch! But even if that's the case, and your heart is set on firms like those, you don't have to transfer. The Job Goddess talked to a number of associates at large firms, themselves graduates of less-than-stellar law schools, and they had an excellent suggestion: a judicial clerkship. As one associate told the Job Goddess, "If you do a federal court clerkship, large law firms will want you, regardless of where you went to school." Apart from increasing your marketability, JH, you would *love* doing a clerkship for a year or two. It's great experience, and many lawyers look back on their clerkships as the most enjoyable part of their career. With your grades, getting a clerkship with a federal judge shouldn't be difficult, and the Job Goddess encourages you to consider that route.

The Job Goddess is probably painting a far worse scenario than actually exists, JH, because it is far more likely that the firms you're eyeing *have* hired people from your school, which means they'll consider you as well. After all, as many recruiting coordinators at large firms have explained to the Job Goddess, often the reason that law firms haven't hired students from certain law schools isn't because they've got something *against* the school—it's just an unknown quantity to them. Once they've got an associate from a school and they like that associate, the way is paved for you to approach that firm.

If you do stick with your school, JH, you've got a lot going for you. Most obviously, you are "the man" or "the woman" (as the case may be). You're a shining star, a Law Review shoo-in, the intellectual center of the universe—and you won't be that anywhere else. Less pragmatically, you've undoubtedly made friends among your classmates and, in all likelihood, probably enjoy your environment. That may or may not be true at any school you transfer to. And while you may be taking a long-term view of your life, you've got another two years left of law school, and there couldn't be a place you'd be more comfortable than you are now. These are perhaps not dispositive issues for you, JH, but they're worth considering, especially with the judicial clerkship option the Job Goddess so firmly favors.

But if the firms you're looking at don't hire from your school (or you've got a class full of schmoes and you can't wait to get away from them, or a judicial clerkship doesn't ring your chimes) such that you *do* decide to transfer, you've got to determine: where to? The two obvious choices are either a law school in the city where you want to live, or a distinguished national school. With the local school option, law firms virtually always hire from local schools, and you can always run a quick Mar-Hub check to see if that's the case. The only problem with this is that as a transferring student, you won't bring your class rank with you, and you won't be able to be on Law Review second year—both of which you'd have if you stayed put. You'd want to list your first-year results very prominently on your resume. Even so, if your grades drop at the new school, you won't have the buffer you have now. As one career services director at a "first-tier" law school told the Job Goddess, "A lot of students transfer here thinking that they're set. They're not. If they're not in the top half of the class here, large firms won't look at them any more quickly than they would have before."

So not all first-tier schools are created equal, JH. Having said that, if you can successfully transfer into a school that anyone would recognize as having a phenomenal reputation, it's hard to come up with solid reasons not to do that—particularly with your large-firm aspirations. As one career services director at a moderately-ranked law school says, "If a student comes to me and says, 'I've got a chance to transfer to Columbia. Should I do it?' I've got a moral obligation to hold out my hand, and say, 'Go. And good luck to you.' The fact is, a degree from Columbia, Yale, or Harvard has cachet that you're going to have for your entire career."

So there you have it, JH. You will notice that throughout this discussion the Job Goddess has not analyzed your stated desire of going to a "large firm." That's a matter for another column, or perhaps a chapter in a book. Suffice it to say that in researching her incredible *America's Greatest Places to Work With a Law Degree*, the Job Goddess has uncovered very few large law firms where junior associates are—dare she say it?—happy. Before you pack your bags and pin your hopes on a generic "large firm," the Job Goddess urges you to talk to alums who work at the firms you're considering joining, to find out from them how they enjoy their jobs—and what you can expect if you follow in their footsteps.

ETERNALLY YOURS,

The Job Goddess

I Got an Interview With a Firm Through a Connection. If They Don't Bring Up My Mediocre Grades... Should I?

Dear Job Goddess,

I got an interview at a huge firm through the husband of a friend of mine. I know they would never have looked at me otherwise because I am nowhere near the top of my class. How do I handle the grades issue, or should I just hope they don't bring it up at all?

RB, Denver

Dear Job Goddess,

Because my last boss was very well connected, I've gotten some interviews with some large firms who would not have interviewed me on campus. Don't get me wrong; I'm in the top third of my class, but these are the kinds of places that only take the top 10%. I am not getting any offers and I'm really frustrated. I think my interviewing style is OK. What am I doing wrong?

CL, Chicago

Dear RB and CL,

You have both unwittingly stumbled onto a dirty little secret of large law firms: namely, the courtesy interview. Of course, the interviews themselves aren't a secret—but the firms' expectations of those interviews normally are.

Here is what is going on for both of you. The firms with whom you have been interviewing are not stupid; when an important client, or mucky-muck of any other stripe, calls and says, "Would you interview my friend/nephew/former secretary/summer intern for an associate position?" the firm is hardly going to respond with a guffaw and a "Yeah, right!" before hanging up the phone. Instead, the firm will say something like, "We'd be delighted to." You get scheduled for an interview, but unbeknownst to you, you have been red-flagged. That is, the lawyers with whom you interview will be told that you are "related to so-and-so" or you "have blackmail photos of so-and-so" (the Job Goddess is just kidding, of course), or whatever your connection may be. What does this mean? It means that the firm believes that it is highly unlikely that your interview will result in further interviews, and—ultimately—an offer.

What do you do? You take that "highly unlikely" and figure out how to turn it to your advantage—with the help of the Job Goddess, of course, and more importantly her friends who have the advice you need. Anne Stark Walker, Career Services Director at the University of Denver College of Law, and before that the hiring partner at a large law firm, says that "If your grades aren't what the firm normally seeks, be sure that you work what you do offer into the conversation. You can say, 'I know I'm not in the part of the class you normally take . . . ' and follow up with what you do have." Like what? As Anne Stark Walker reports, "It is always possible to wow them with personality and work experience. So if you have any work experience before or during law school, make the most of that. Firms are more and more conscious of how much it costs to train new associates, and the fact that they can't bill clients for training time. That puts pressure on new associates to hit the ground running. So if you can show them that, because you have prior work experience, especially servicing clients, that counts."

What if you don't have prior work experience? Says Walker, "Regardless of any experience you have, it's important to impress the firm with your maturity and savvy. The lawyers with whom you interview will be asking themselves: How do you handle yourself? Are you poised? Can you easily field questions? Can you carry the conversational ball without constantly needing to be prodded? Can you talk about things you've done by way of telling anecdotes?" What does all of this add up to, RB and CL? You can overcome not having phenomenal grades by showing great interpersonal skills. Anne Walker advises, "Show them that you are bright, energetic, and enthusiastic. You wouldn't be the first successful associate who originally got a foot in the door with a courtesy interview. The fact is that firms want 10 degrees more enthusiasm more than they want a top-10 student with no commitment. If you show that you are hungrier for the job, that is a point in your favor."

What if you can't get past the order-of-the-coif bias, even if you've got the interviewing skills of Larry King and Barbara Walters all rolled into one? As Anne Walker points out, "At the very worst, if you show enthusiasm and interview well, you can make great connections. If you click with a lawyer at a firm and they like you, they will pass your name onto somebody else, and that somebody else could well wind up making you an offer."

So what is it that tanks most courtesy interviewees? They don't do all of the things the Job Goddess has just discussed, RB and CL. They hope against hope that the grades issue won't come up, or believe that if the firm doesn't bring up grades that the grades don't matter. They don't research the employer up front. They don't think of experiences, paid or volunteer, law-related or not, that show that they've got skills valuable to the firm or can learn those skills quickly. They don't look at the firm's web page or get familiar with what they do or smile or ask questions or rehearse answers to questions they know they'll get, all of which the Job Goddess covers in the interviewing chapter of her fabulous bestseller, *Guerrilla Tactics for Getting the Legal Job of Your Dreams*.

But now that you know what you're up against, RB and CL, you know the prep work you have to do to turn those "connected" interviews into gold!

ETERNALLY YOURS,

The Job Goddess

Grown-Up Problems

Second Careerers and
"Students of the Night"

Handling Attitudes Towards "Law Students of the Night"

Dear Job Goddess,

I work full-time, and go to law school in the evening. I've heard that there is a decided prejudice against "law students of the night," and I wonder if this is true.

MH, Washington

Dear MH,

The Job Goddess has heard many queries like yours, MH, but you're the first to thoughtfully provide her with the "law students of the night" gag. Although you didn't say it in so many words, you actually have two questions. After all, you're not so much concerned with whether or not this prejudice exists; that would require a very short reply. "Yes, it does," or "No, it doesn't. Thanks for writing." What's more important is, if it does exist, what do you do about it? The Job Goddess has already tipped her hand on the existence of this prejudice by expanding your question this way, but the good news is that you can easily turn a potential problem to your advantage.

As to the existence of an evening student prejudice, the Job Goddess checked around to see if it's true that employers view evening students as sneetches who lack stars on their bellies (if you don't recognize the reference, check back through your Dr. Seuss library). Much as the Job Goddess dislikes admitting it, there are, in fact, employers who view evening students as career-ically challenged—primarily employers who aren't educated about evening programs. (Gee, funny how prejudice works that way.) Amy Berenson, Career Services Director at the UCLA Law School, has done extensive research on evening programs. She says, "The problem for evening students involves more ignorance than prejudice. Some employers don't know about night school, and since it's different than what they themselves did, they tend to view it suspiciously." The misperceptions seem to involve two primary areas. First, that evening programs are easier to get into than day programs, and so the quality of students is lower. The other is that the evening professors are of lower quality than day professors, and therefore the quality of education that night students get is lower.

In a nutshell, MH, employers who look askance at evening programs seem to envision a law degree that you got by responding to a matchbook that reads, "You too can be a lawyer!"

So, yes, MH, some employers will look askance at your program. But that doesn't make you legal employment roadkill. To mix metaphors in a horrible way, MH, now that the cat is out of the bag, let's look at the multiple ways you can skin it. Amy Berenson suggests one method, which involves focusing your job search on kindred spirits. "Call or visit your career services office, and identify evening student alumni." Make these people the first ones you contact; if you solicit their advice, you know you'll find a sympathetic ear and useful resource, because they themselves have been there and done that. Furthermore, any employer who has hired evening students in the past, from any law school, won't suffer under the false image you fear. As Mary Beth Daisy, Assistant Director of Career Services at Rutgers University/Camden School of Law, points out, "Employers who've hired evening students know their advantages. They don't have to adjust to a work environment, they know how to balance responsibilities, they have a whole variety of skills because of what they've been through."

Another method for overcoming the night school prejudice involves attacking the misperception head-on, and selling the advantages you have over full-time day students. First, don't be shy about disabusing people—in a nice way—of any wrongheaded notions about your program, both as to the quality of the students and the quality of the professors. As Amy Berenson points out, "The admissions standard for evening programs is no different than day programs. In fact, the qualifications students need to get into night programs are sometimes higher than for the day division. And the night curriculum is just as vigorous as it is during the day, and the classes are taught by the same faculty." You can always soften these points by stating them in terms of a general misperception, instead of pointing the finger at the employer you're talking to. You can say something like, "You know, a lot of people don't realize that it's actually more difficult (or just as difficult, whichever applies) to get into the evening division than the day division. . . . " In short, you've got to convince them that the difference between night and day isn't night and day!

On top of setting the record straight, you'll want to sell everything you've got that a day division student typically wouldn't have. As Amy Berenson points out, "You've had to juggle responsibilities, and you should sell that! You've got the discipline, commitment, and skills from your full-time work environment that full-time students lack. Look at the personal qualities you have as a result of taking on all of your responsibilities. It's not about someone who can't get into the day program!"

The Job Goddess is certain that either of these approaches will work for you, MH. After all, as the Job Goddess frequently points out, there simply is no flaw, real or perceived, that can prevent you from snagging your dream job. The key is how you present yourself, the words you use to sell what you've got. As the Job Goddess has seen borne out over and over again, if you use confident language in describing what you bring to the table, employers will adopt your attitude and have confidence in you as well.

ETERNALLY YOURS,

The Job Goddess

GI Joe Turns Lawyer—How to Translate Military Experience Into Civilian Language

Dear Job Goddess,

I am a Captain in the U.S. Army, currently serving on active duty. I go to law school at night, after duty hours. How do I translate my military experience (e.g., Company Commander) into language a legal recruiter will understand and appreciate?

GW, Graham, Washington

Dear GW,

How wise of you to grasp a problem many legal employers encounter. Faced with the resume of a military person who may very well be a dream employee, they just don't know what to make of experience like

"X-4 Officer on Flux Capacitor Transmogrification Program, responsible for WY Velocity Vector Group." So as you correctly surmise, GW, it's not so much a matter of what you've done that counts—virtually any career gives you skills that will benefit you as a lawyer. It's how you say it. And this isn't just true for law—it's true for anything. You may have heard the story about Satchel Paige, perhaps the best baseball pitcher ever. Well, as a kid, he was in reform school, and since he was kind of scrawny, he defended himself by throwing rocks. It turns out he could throw them with stinging accuracy. And one day, a grownup came up to him, put a paternal hand on his shoulder, and said, "Son, you shouldn't be throwing rocks. You should be throwing baseballs." Voila! Transferable skill—from juvenile delinquent to star pitcher. For you, GW, to the extent you make it easy for legal employers to understand what you bring to the table from your military experience, you'll be rewarded with job offers you might have deserved, but wouldn't otherwise receive.

Let's see exactly how you do this. As Amy Berenson, Career Services Director at the UCLA Law School, advises, "You have to go beyond your title, and look at the skills you learned that would be applicable in a civilian environment. For instance, let's say that you've had to work as a member of a group to accomplish tasks. That proven ability to be a team player is valuable to many legal employers. Also, look at what you've done and identify if you've had to organize projects, juggle conflicting responsibilities, create a budget, or train people—things like that. Those are all skills that will generate interest in you from civilian employers."

To accomplish this, GW, practice! Imagine that you're actually talking to a civilian you want to work for, and you have to give them the reasons why they should hire you. You've got to make the connection for them; think about what it is you'd do if you worked for this employer, and how your experience translates into the ability to do, or quickly learn, those tasks. Use wording like, "In the army, I did X, and this shows that I can do Y for you." Saying that you've attained the rank of Captain isn't, by itself, meaningful to civilians—at least, not civilians like the Job Goddess, whose woeful lack of knowledge of the military ends pretty much with her observation that virtually everybody looks great in uniform. But let's say that making it all the way to captain has required you to supervise increasing numbers of people. Well, as Amy Berenson points out, supervising people is a leadership skill that's valuable to legal employers, regardless of where you learned it. And you'd want to go further and state the number of people you've supervised. Numbers are something anyone can grasp, while saying you led a "platoon" or a "company" isn't.

You'd also, of course, want to highlight any technical skills you've learned that would be relevant to the kind of career you're after. For instance, if your military work involves the use of computers, that's a skill that many legal employers covet. Or perhaps your experience has given you scientific knowledge that would be useful to an intellectual property practice. Or maybe you've become familiar with an industry that forms the client base for a certain specialty. Whatever your experience is, GW, it might give you a particular expertise that you can easily sell to appropriate civilian employers.

Beyond the way you sell your skills to employers in general, GW, the Job Goddess feels compelled to point out that in terms of the specific employers you contact, you can turn your military experience into a real plus by going after employers who have a military background themselves. You'll find that your common experience will be an instant source of connection for you, and that's always a plus. How do you find these people? As Amy Berenson suggests, "Go through an on-line directory like Martindale-Hubbell, looking specifically for lawyers with a military background. You may also want to contact the Pentagon and ask them for databases or profiles that show you the same thing." Also, if you've got technical expertise, look at civilian employers in specialties and industries who would find that valuable—again, your career services office, or a reference librarian, can identify the resources you'd use to pinpoint those employers. And when you contact those employers, make sure that the first thing you mention—and the item on the top of your resume!—is the facet of your military experience that will make you uniquely valuable to them.

By the way, the problem you describe is not limited to people with a military background, GW. Anyone with a career in something a legal employer can't readily grasp faces your difficulty. For instance, the Job Goddess met a woman who had been a nuclear physicist for years before attending law school. She had a lengthy resume, consisting, as far as the Job Goddess could decipher, entirely of scientific terms lacking any vowels whatsoever. When you think about it, the fact that you've done something that's not immediately obvious is a plus; it's complex enough to require an explanation. After all, if you'd spent 10 years working the drive-thru window at the Burger Emperor, any employer would know what that means, and what it says about you— once they stopped laughing, that is. So the fact that you've got to take a bit of time to explain what you bring to the table says something wonderful about you—make the most of it!

ETERNALLY YOURS,

The Job Goddess

—*∞*—

Law as a Second Career: Handling the "Why Law?" Question

Dear Job Goddess,

I recently graduated from law school and passed the bar. Before law school, I spent a number of years as a secondary school teacher. Whenever I talk to employers, it seems they are interested in my teaching experience and want to know why I left that career. Why do you think there is this fascination? Should I even continue to include this information on my resume? It has been seven years since I got out of teaching and I have been in the legal environment completely since that time. What do you suggest, Job Goddess?

LS, Boston

Dear LS,

Ah, you are going to be delighted when you discover the simple solution to your predicament. *Everybody* who worked before law school—and that's a lot of people—faces the "why law?" issue. So let's talk about what you're up against and how to turn it to your greatest advantage.

When an employer asks you about your prior career, there are, at first glance, two basic alternative responses. Either you were a real loser as a teacher, and nobody wants to hire a refugee from a bad career. Or you were a *terrific* teacher, which will call into question your decision-making ability, not to mention your credibility. In between, there are a whole raft of ill-thought-out, flip answers that "second-careerers" give when asked about their prior lives. The pantheon of truly horrible experiences include "I took the LSAT on a dare," "I've always been good at arguing," "I really like *L.A. Law* (or John Grisham books)," or the response that curdles an interviewer's blood—*"I wanted to make more money."* As a rule of thumb, if you would not feel comfortable breaking wind in an interview—and the Job Goddess trusts you would *not*—then do not discuss money there, either.

So, what *should* you do, LS? First of all, de-fang the interviewer. You're not under attack. In the interviewer's shoes, you'd be naturally curious about that prior career, too. With that in mind, how do you characterize your prior career to enhance your chances of receiving an offer? The two keys here are "Stressing a long-term interest in the law, and pulling the transferable skills from your prior career," according to Diane Ballou, Director of Career Services at the University of Connecticut School of Law.

First, the long-term-interest element helps you dispel the notion that you're jumping into the law blind. A long, slow deliberation about your career change helps you immensely. Stress any experience you've had that exposed you to what you'd *really* do as a lawyer. For instance, the career of a relative or acquaintance, or a relevant clinic, class or volunteer work, would fit the bill, where watching old Perry Mason reruns *wouldn't*.

Second, the transferable skills element accomplishes two things for you. For a start, it shows that you really know what you're getting into; after all, you can't show what you're bringing to the table unless you know something about that table first. Diane Ballou, herself a school teacher in a prior life, points out that teaching is an excellent background for law, if you pull out the right assets. She lists some of the best ones: "Teaching gives you experience standing in front of people, which makes you good on your feet, an excellent skill for lawyers. Furthermore, since teachers don't have anyone looking over their shoulder most of the time, you're good at working independently. And apart from writing and verbal skills that all legal employers covet, you're good at explaining things to people. That means you'll be good at reducing complex legal ideas to a level clients can understand."

You get the gist here, LS; you're not characterizing yourself as a teacher or tailor or candlestick-maker who went into law. Rather, you're showing the lawyering *skills* you're "pre-programmed" with as a result of your prior experience. And of course it would behoove you to do the same thing for any hobbies, part-time jobs, or any other kind of experience you have. *Always* think of yourself in terms of the skills you bring forward for your next employer, not what you technically *did* for your last employer.

Finally, please *don't* upset the Job Goddess by suggesting you might lift your teaching career from your resume, leaving a gap of many years. You know, LS, that when employers see a gap in a resume, they assume the worst. Prison. Drug rehab. Witness protection program. Ugh! Much, much better to restructure your resume, as Diane Ballou suggests, on a "functional" basis, stressing functions you can perform over particular jobs you've held. (If you need to know more about resumes, the Job Goddess is shamelessly delighted to refer you to her fabulous bestseller, *Guerrilla Tactics for Getting the Legal Job of Your Dreams*, which has a great chapter on resumes—and everything else, for that matter.)

So fear not, LS. Practice the words that show why "LS-former-teacher" will now be "LS-terrific-lawyer." The Job Goddess promises you that you will be delighted by the reactions you receive.

ETERNALLY YOURS,

The Job Goddess

If I Work All Day and Go to Law School at Night, How Do I Make the "Jump" Into Law?

DEAR JOB GODDESS,

*I am a second-year evening student in a four-year program in Los Angeles. I currently work for the county health services department, inspecting radioactive materials users in L.A.County. I like my job, but I would like to start to put my legal education to work somewhere. Should I get out into the "real law world" before graduation? And if so, how? I realize I'll probably make less than I do now, but hopefully not **much** less.*

BH, Los Angeles

DEAR BH,

The Job Goddess marvels at **anybody** like you, BH, who can work full time **and** attend law school at night. The Job Goddess herself had her hands full with a simple full-time course load at law school, but then a steady diet of 25-cent draft beers and buffalo chicken wings may not have helped her stamina.

In the Job Goddess's experience talking with evening law students, she has encountered four broad categories of people. First, those who intend to use their law degree to move into the legal department where they work; second, people who want to parlay their experience and their law degree into a law practice of their own; third, people who don't want to stay where they are but have a definite idea of what kind of work they want to do; and finally, people who don't have any idea what they want to do when they get their degree, but hope that whatever it is will bring them great satisfaction and, not incidentally, buckets o' cash.

Let's say that you fit the first category, BH, and want to stay pretty much where you are, but do legal work as well. Talk with people where you work and find out who handles legal issues, whether there is an in-house legal department, or whether all work is farmed out to law firms. If everything is done in-house, make yourself known to everybody in that department. Get to know them, find out about the work they do, and offer to help out researching issues or handling projects in your spare time (the Job Goddess realizing that "spare time" is a relative term). Let them know that your goal in going to law school was to expand your horizons, and that while you enjoy the work you do, you'd like to stretch your skills by helping them out, too. Find out about when they have job openings and how, when you graduate, you might go about getting one. The Job Goddess has found that the problem most people have in this kind of situation is that they feel it's too bold to talk to people in the legal department this way. But if you put yourself in their shoes, BH, you can see that what you're doing is very flattering; you're saying, "I want to be like you." And people inevitably respond positively to that kind of attention.

If it turns out that working in-house isn't feasible, find out which law firm handles work for your employer, and get to know *them* through lawyers who are in-house. Because you work for a client, your employer's law firm will certainly be open to, at the very least, meeting with you so that you can learn more about the field and discover new and valuable contacts.

Another viable option might be to combine the expertise you have with the law degree you're soon to have, and hang out your own shingle. This is a very popular route for evening students, and with good reason:

they typically have a built-in potential client base as a result of their daytime career. While this is far too large a topic to tackle in this one column, if you haven't considered it before, it's worth thinking about. After all, when it comes to potential, as your own boss there's no limit to the amount of money you can make.

But let's switch hats, BH, and pretend you're in the third group; that is, you know what you want to do with your law degree, and it's not what you're doing now. It's actually very easy for you to get your feet wet even with your intense schedule. How? Go to your career services office, and find out who runs the specialty section for the specialty you want to get into at the local bar. Start reading local bar newsletters and keep up with who's doing what in the legal world via your local newspaper (assuming you want to stay where you are). Go to the specialty bar meetings, lunches, seminars, anything that you can fit into your schedule. Introduce yourself to people, learn about what they do, and when they ask about *you*, explain to them that you'd like to do some freelance work to gain experience in the specialty you want to enter, and offer to research issues, write briefs, whatever you can do *on your own time*. Make this known to the attorney who runs your specialty section for the local bar association, to see if any members have stated a need for freelance help, and also to see if you can do any projects for the local bar itself to gain experience. Certain kinds of practices, of course, *do* have office hours that could accommodate you. For instance, legal aid offices are typically open at night and on weekends, and you might be able to work there if that interests you. Again, by doing these kinds of activities, you are getting to know the right people and learning about jobs you'll want, so that you'll be perfectly situated to make that jump when you've got your degree.

Now if you're in the final group, and you just don't know what you want to do (but you know it's not what you're doing now), you've got to do a bit of exploratory work before you jump into ***anything***. As Bernice Davenport, Career Services Director at Thomas Cooley Law School, suggests, "I always advise evening students to spend their first year focusing on academics. Then, in year two, it's time to start putting feelers out, just in the sense of learning what's out there. Read legal newspapers and magazines, which your career services office will stock. Call your local bar association, and find out what kinds of activities they have, and what you can fit into your schedule." Go to those events, listen to speakers, and talk with people who already practice law, being very frank about your desire to learn more so that you can plot a career path for yourself. If you feel at all reticent about this, remember that every practicing attorney was once a law student, too, and many of them—primarily the miserable ones—wish they'd done the kind of footwork you're doing! Once you've identified a specialty you like, go ahead and pursue the kinds of activities the Job Goddess has already discussed; volunteering for freelance projects and the like.

Incidentally, BH, the Job Goddess applauds you for your acknowledgement of the possibility of a pay cut when you start law. It is one of the cruel ironies of law that very experienced, highly-qualified people in other fields get a law degree assuming it will enhance their income potential, only to find that they are looking at jobs making less—sometimes considerably less—than they are used to. While getting a law degree needn't mean a new diet of deviled ham and Spam on a Ritz, it's important to recognize that you may have to take a step back in order to make a giant leap forward in the near future. And you may find, as many evening students do, that the value of pursuing what you really want—typically in the form of a public interest position, but not always—provides in psychic income what is lost in the hard green stuff.

So ultimately, BH, what is the Job Goddess suggesting? That it's not really a jump you're making at all, but a series of bunny hops that amount to a jump. By taking the steps outlined here, you're gradually submerging yourself in your new career, making sure every step of the way that you're getting into something you really will enjoy. And with all of the sacrifices you've made, you deserve it!

ETERNALLY YOURS,

The Job Goddess

What's Out There?

Lawyer as Lion-Tamer or: What Else Can I Do With My Law Degree?

Dear Job Goddess,

My real problem is that I don't want to be an attorney. I do not know what exactly I do want to do, though. I got my law degree because I think law is fascinating. But now what? I want to use my degree somehow, but more than that, I want a normal 40-hours-per-week job and vacation time. I would appreciate any suggestions you have, Job Goddess.

KP, Michigan

Dear Job Goddess,

I go to law school part-time at night, and during the day I work in a non-legal field. I enjoy studying law, but I'm beginning to think the first-year associate track may not be for me. I am desperately seeking information on anything nontraditional. Are there any options out there, Job Goddess?

PW, Philadelphia

Dear Job Goddess,

I have contacted seemingly 89 bazillion firms, companies, organizations, etc., looking for a job in technology law/policy. I have good work experience, but on the "not-so-stellar" side, my grades are less than wonderful. I know that I can do a great job for someone given the opportunity, but I am facing some real obstacles getting that opportunity. Any advice?

MG, Winston-Salem

DEAR JOB GODDESS,

I'm a second year and I have decided I just don't want to be a practicing attorney. Can you give me any advice on alternative careers?

SK, San Diego

DEAR KP, PW, MG, SK, E-I-E-I-O

(the latter representing everybody else in the same boat, whose queries the Job Goddess didn't quote),

Of course the Job Goddess has some ideas for you! The Job Goddess herself, after all, has a law degree, and you'd hardly call goddessing 'practicing law.' But since there is only room for one Job Goddess, presumably you want something else. And how, you ponder, do you find it? Remember, the Job Goddess *always* delivers. And that means she *will* lead you to some really fabulous, off-the-beaten track opportunities. As Mary Obrzut, the Director of Career Services of Northern Illinois University College of Law points out, "There are jobs out there that'll knock your socks off."

But first, let's figure out what's stumping all of you. One possibility is that you know the kinds of things you *like* to do, and figure that any want ad that starts with the words "Law Review, top 10%" won't fit the bill. The other possibility is that you don't know what you like to do, but you know it's not the traditional associate route. Either way, you're going to wind up deliriously happy.

There's just a difference in technique when it comes to the route you'll take, that's all.

All rightey then. Let's start with the easy one: you know what you like but just don't know where to look for unconventional stuff. You're *really* in luck. Three gold mines of offbeat jobs that Mary Obrzut recommends are these: First, *Attorney Jobs: The National and Federal Legal & Employment Report*. As Mary Obrzut describes it, this monthly newsletter has all kinds of interesting jobs, here and abroad, with the connecting thread being that they all require a J.D. "If you want something exotic, like American Samoa," says Mary Obrzut, "This is the newsletter to check out." It's published by Federal Reports, Inc., P.O. Box 3709, Georgetown Station, Washington, D.C. 20007. The phone number is 800-296-9611.

Second, there's a biweekly newsletter called *Opportunities in Public Affairs*. This covers jobs as everything from legislative assistants on Capitol Hill, to interns at CNN, to government affairs jobs, to print and broadcast journalism jobs. Again, all ones where a J.D. is a plus. To subscribe, write to P.O. Box 34949, Bethesda, MD 20827, or call 301-571-0102.

And finally, there's the biweekly *Environmental Career Opportunities* newspaper. Mary Obrzut describes this one as containing "everything from attorneys for wildlife, health, and nonprofits, to camp counseling jobs." To get it, write to P.O. Box 560, Stanardsville, VA 22973, or call 301-320-2002.

Now, what about the other problem? What if you just don't know what you like? Well, getting these three wonderful newsletters is a start; it may well be that you just need a bit of off-beat inspiration to flip your career switch. But if it's more than that—if you really don't know what you want—take heart. You're not alone. The Job Goddess's own response to "What are you going to do with your degree?" for her entire law school career could be summarized by the word, "duh." The fact is, if you don't know the kinds of things you like to do, you've *got* to figure that out before you can pursue *anything*. I know, I know. Every law student hates the touchy-feely who-am-I-if-I-were-a-color-what-color-would-I-be-who-invented-liquid-soap-and-why type questions you probably think you've got to endure. But it's really not that bad. Really. And besides, without some clue as to how you like to fill your time, neither the Job Goddess nor anyone could hand you a card with a job on it, and ensure that you'd enjoy it—because your enjoyment depends on what you uniquely like to do. So you do have to rattle your own internal cage, first.

How do you do that? Well, there are a number of pretty simple ways. One is to visit your career services office at school; there are any number of simple tests to help you figure out what kinds of activities suit you. Another option—shameless commercial plug time—is to read the second chapter of the Job Goddess's fabulous book, *Guerrilla Tactics for Getting the Legal Job of Your Dreams*, which is all about deciding on your dream job. OK, OK, you don't have to buy it; it's at every career services office at every law school in the country, and it's at a lot of law libraries as well. It's a pretty long chapter, but then, when you're choosing a path that's going to make you happy forever, that's worth a little bit of spade work, *n'est pas*? Without bogging you down with specifics here, the chapter gives you all kinds of quizzes and questions that bring to light what kinds of activities make you happy—outside of considerations of salary, and prestige, and what your professors, parents, family, or classmates tell you that you *ought* to want, and forgetting for a moment about what you think you can get. (The Job Goddess knows you can get *anything* you want.) The Job Goddess's experience, talking with law students all over the country, is that you really, secretly *do* know the kinds of things you like to do—it's just that law school has beaten your dreams out of you. You just need a little nudge to revivify them. And that's what the Job Goddess lives for!

ETERNALLY YOURS,

The Job Goddess

I Want to Work a Forty-Hour Week. Am I Dreaming?

DEAR JOB GODDESS,

When I graduate, I want a job that comes as close to a 40-hour work week as I can reasonably get. I'm not afraid of hard work, but I have a family and I don't want to be penalized for it. Is there such a thing in the legal field?

Although I don't live in a big city, the bigger firms we have treat you like they own you. I don't want to be treated like a juvenile and I also don't want to start at $30,000 a year. Is there any hope?

SJ, Syracuse

DEAR SJ,

Of course there is hope, SJ; the Job Goddess never says otherwise. Let's see what you ought to consider doing.

First, however, the Job Goddess feels compelled to defend the bigger law firms you condemn. Simply put, in law, the words "hard work" are a euphemism for "long hours." When law firms tell you they work hard, it doesn't mean that they hew stone into legal briefs. It means that, like Dracula, they eschew daylight. Some simple economics explain why the big bucks of large firms come at a big price.

If you start at $80,000, that means that as a rule of thumb the firm will have to charge clients about $240,000 to cover your salary, benefits, overhead, profit, and so on. If they bill you out at, say, $100 an hour, they've got to bill out 2400 hours on you for a year. And if you add an average 300 hours a year for training, interviewing, and so on, and tack on an additional 20% for time you blow at work on talking with colleagues and other nonbillable time, you're talking a six-day week at 11 hours a day. Of course firms don't all follow this exact formula, but it does show that the "sweatshop" atmosphere of many firms is directly traceable to the bucks they pay. And that is, of course, why many large firm associates say that what they really have are two $40,000-a-year jobs.

So much for the bad news. The good news? If you don't want to dance, don't go to the prom. The Job Goddess consulted with Laura Rowe Lane, Assistant Career Services Director at the George Washington University School of Law, for some ideas more along the lines of what you want, SJ.

For instance, in private practice, you could consider working for a large firm on a part-time basis. As Laura Rowe Lane points out, "Many large firms offer part-time and flex-time work, but many people don't take them up on it." Even on a part-time basis the pay is good, and so are the benefits.

You could also be a contract attorney for a larger firm. As a contract attorney you sign on for a project for a period of time, say between six months and two years (and you can do this over and over again). Laura Rowe Lane says that, "You can get one aspect of a case, like discovery, or a whole project. You might get benefits, and the pay is typically attractive, between $20 and $45 an hour." Although you don't want to be an associate at a large firm, SJ, many contract associates *are* invited to stay as permanent associates by the firms they work for.

You could also consider smaller firms, which typically require fewer hours, but the pay is commensurately less. The $30,000 salary you're trying to avoid wouldn't be an unusual starting point for a smaller firm, but it's important to note that where you *start* doesn't say anything about what you'll make in six months or a year. You can up the ante by negotiating for a salary plus a portion of the business you bring in, or a bonus based on cases you win (if you want to litigate). If you have questions about whether the hours at a given firm really are what you're looking for, you can typically "Smoke it out from associates," says Laura Rowe Lane. Or you can do your own detective work. If a firm tells you it expects a 40-hour week from its associates, and you call or stop by at 6:30 p.m. and the attorneys are still there, they're probably not putting in a 40-hour week, no matter what they tell you.

You might consider avoiding a firm altogether by freelancing for many small firms. You can do research or write briefs, for instance. This works because the workload of many sole practitioners and small firms is unpredictable, so they can't take on a full-time associate but may have plenty of projects for freelancers. Or, as Laura Rowe Lane suggests, you could latch onto just one sole practitioner who needs help; she knows a law school graduate with small children who works from 9 a.m. to 2 p.m. for a lawyer, and tends her children the rest of the time. And the Job Goddess knows of women law graduates with family concerns who ensure a reasonable week by banding together and opening their own firms straight out of law school. It lacks security, to be sure, but makes up for that in autonomy and excitement. If you have an entrepreneurial bent and similar-minded friends, it might be an idea for you.

You may also consider clerking for a judge. Clerkship hours are typically very attractive, and most judicial clerks love their jobs—interesting work, schmoozing with judges, getting great respect from lawyers—it's a great life. Court administration jobs, like being a staff attorney as opposed to clerking for a particular judge, is also a great alternative, if doing legal research rings your chimes.

Oh, SJ, the Job Goddess could go on and on. Working as an attorney for a trade association, or designing web sites for law firms . . . the jobs with reasonable hours are plentiful. The Job Goddess happens to know all about this, because, while researching *America's Greatest Places to Work With a Law Degree*, she found that reasonable hours are one of the most important attributes of a dream job.

So there is more than hope of finding a great job that won't own you—there's a big, bold, inviting reality!

ETERNALLY YOURS,

The Job Goddess

Casting Your Bread Upon the Waters

How to Get to Employers Without
Cover Letters or Resumes

How Do I Network My Way Into the CIA?

Dear Job Goddess,

Everybody, including you, always talks about networking this, networking that. I have always wanted to work for the CIA. Now that I am in law school, it's time for me to seriously start my campaign. But how do I network my way in when I can't even find out who works there?

Stumped,

EJ, Missouri

Dear EJ,

At the outset the Job Goddess would like to compliment you on your outstanding career choice, EJ. The CIA figures prominently in the Job Goddess's new book—warning: unforgivable self-promotion ahead—*America's Greatest Places to Work With a Law Degree.* Lawyers *love* working at the CIA. There's huge variety and the Job Goddess understands that if you want to get into—ahem—***non-lawyer*** work at the CIA, you periodically have that opportunity. And incidentally, the CIA has a very interesting web page, at www.odci.gov/cia/. There's even a kiddie page. It's well worth a visit even if you have no intention of CIA-ing it after school.

So! Your question, EJ. I'm hunching that you think you've flummoxed the Job Goddess, and for people who aren't familiar with breaking into the CIA—the Job Goddess is speaking metaphorically, of course—here, in a nutshell, is EJ's problem. The CIA does not make public who its employees are. And so your traditional sources of making contact—namely, going to your alumni services director at school and asking, "Do we have any graduates at the CIA?" won't work. All right, all right, the Job Goddess acknowledges that this is a problem. But it doesn't mean that you can't find people at the CIA via *any* means. What you want to do is hack your way into . . .

Just kidding.

The Job Goddess spoke with lawyers at the CIA, and posed them your question. They had this advice for you, EJ:

"For informal contact with the CIA, there are several methods you might try. The most obvious is to ask everybody you know whether they know anybody who works for the CIA. All of us are frequently contacted by children of friends of friends who want to know about working for the CIA, and we always talk with them. You'd be surprised how many people get to us that way. Another possibility is to keep an eye on speakers who come to your school. The CIA regularly sends out people to talk on law school campuses, and at job fairs." One option would be to contact the CIA's public affairs department to find out where, and when, they will have attorneys visiting law schools. If they will be anywhere in your vicinity, EJ, it would be worth making a phone call to the career services director at the host school and asking whether you can attend. The Job Goddess assures you that career services directors respond *very* well to enthusiasm, and so you will undoubtedly be invited to attend. And when you *go*, the Job Goddess need scarcely mention that you should be sure to hang around afterwards and chat with the speaker in person. The Job Goddess can attest from her own vast experience visiting law schools that the one element that makes such visits most worthwhile is talking with law students afterwards.

And incidentally, as is true with every job in the universe, it is very worthwhile having somebody on the inside pulling for you, even if it is simply a matter of your new-found contact walking over to the person who hires summer clerks or new attorneys and saying, "I met this guy when I spoke at his school, and I think we ought to bring him in for an interview." That's a real boost—and would vault you out of the stack of applications in the in-box.

So while "networking"—ugh, the Job Goddess hates that word—through alums or published directories isn't a possibility, there are a number of ways to make the contacts you desire, EJ. The Job Goddess is confident that you will be outfitted with a shoe phone and magic decoder ring before you know it.

ETERNALLY YOURS,

The Job Goddess

How Do I Get Into the Expensive Conferences Where My Dream Employers Are?

Dear Job Goddess,

My boyfriend wants to go into Securities Law. We found out about a seminar being given next month in New York City on securities law, and obviously there will be many securities practitioners there. We think it would be a great opportunity but it costs over a thousand dollars! He is a recent law school grad, awaiting bar results . . . in other words, he's broke! What do you think about calling people associated with the event and asking if he could do some volunteer work in exchange for the cost of the program? I thought this would be a great excuse to speak with some of these potential employers and show some enthusiasm. Please help. He really needs the motivation!

CE, Michigan

Dear CE,

Why, CE, your boyfriend should kiss the ground you walk on, if he doesn't do so already. You have unwittingly stumbled upon one of the Job Goddess's most beloved means of getting a great job.

Why is that? Because volunteering at the kind of event you describe accomplishes several very important goals. One is that it attacks the problem that 90% of legal jobs are never advertised. The practitioners you describe are the gatekeepers for these kinds of jobs; they will know about them even though you currently don't. Furthermore, volunteering overcomes the greatest obstacle facing most job seekers. Everybody wants a job search to be a paper chase (or, more modernly, the Job Goddess supposes, a cyber chase). But the fact is that people hire people. When you make yourself into a flesh-and-blood human being as opposed to a bunch o' credentials on a page, you increase one hundredfold your chances of nailing down a great job, because people hire *people*, not credentials. The Job Goddess has seen over and over again that if an employer likes you as a person, that employer will come up with excuses to hire you over those who look far better on paper. Furthermore, by volunteering, you are correct in surmising that your boyfriend will exhibit his enthusiasm—the single most desirable character trait in the minds of employers. If the people your boyfriend meets at this seminar view him as a go-getter—and the Job Goddess is certain they will—then he will be the one they naturally think of when they come across job opportunities in that giant, hidden job market.

Volunteering also overcomes a serious obstacle facing most law students, and that is the dislike of talking to strangers. Studies show that 85% of people dislike talking to strangers, and in the case of law students facing lawyers, that dislike is understandable. The Job Goddess remembers contemplating professional meetings when she was a law student, and dismissing them with the thought that, as a law student, she would have nothing to say to practitioners. By volunteering, you have a role to play, whether it's making out nametags, pouring the punch, answering the phone, whatever. And when you have a role to play, the ice is broken, and conversation flows naturally.

In fact, in her fairly constant wanderings to law schools around the country, the Job Goddess has met many, many students who have turned simple volunteering opportunities to gold. One standout is a student who wanted to get into aviation law. He got onto mailing lists for aviation law practitioners, and discovered a weekend conference that he wanted to attend. His problem was the same as your boyfriend's, CE—the conference cost a thousand dollars. So he called the conference organizer, described his predicament, and offered to help out in return for free admission. His specific offering was a stroke of genius; he volunteered to drive to the conference, some three hundred miles away, and ferry conference attendees from the airport to the conference site. Well, CE, you can imagine what those conversations in his car were like! "As a matter of fact, I'm still in law school. I'm here to learn more about aviation law, because it's what I really want to do." When he excitedly told the Job Goddess about this, he said that, "I was the only law student there, with hundreds of aviation lawyers from all over the country. I don't know where exactly I want to settle down, but no matter where it is, I already know somebody there!"

Another student, this one a young woman who wanted to get into international law, had similarly spectacular results. By reading the local papers she found that the Summit of American States was going to take place in the city where she attended law school. She called and volunteered to help out, and wound up acting as an assistant to the executive director of the conference. At the conference, she met a couple of U.S. Senators. One of them offered her an internship in his office. At his office, she met someone who offered her a vacation job at the White House. And at the White House, she met someone who offered her a summer clerkship at a U.S. Embassy in the Caribbean. Great grades? No. Built-in contacts? No. ***Great initiative?*** Absolutely.

Clearly, CE, your boyfriend has already cottoned onto this idea. If the Job Goddess's hunch is correct—and it usually is—he has already made the important first step of getting onto mailing lists for newsletters involving his chosen specialty, and reads trade publications to see what's going on. This is the very best, and easiest, way to find out about professional meetings like seminars and conferences. While law school encourages a kind of tunnel vision, obtaining a great job requires looking outside and finding meetings and conferences that are not only professionally useful, but interesting and fun to attend. From there, as you have already figured out, CE, it's a simple matter of contacting the organizer of the meeting or conference, and offering one's services in return for free attendance. This frequently hits pay dirt because virtually every meeting or conference needs volunteers, and having one extra body—that of your enthusiastic boyfriend—doesn't contribute one additional cent to overhead costs.

Oh, CE, the Job Goddess could clearly wax on and on about what a good idea you've stumbled upon. Yes, yes,

yes, encourage your boyfriend to volunteer his services at the securities seminar. And have him treat you to a lavish vacation when he nails down his dream job as a result—you deserve it!

ETERNALLY YOURS,

The Job Goddess

Setting the Hook

Headhunters, Job Ads,
and Cover Letters

Is It OK to Use E-Mail When I'm Looking for a Job With a Law Firm?

Dear Job Goddess,

Ever since I started using e-mail I've forgotten how to stick stamps on envelopes (well, almost). It seems to me that it would be so much easier to e-mail cover letters and resumes to law firms rather than to send these via snail mail, especially since so many law firms now have web sites that let you e-mail them directly. How do employers feel about this?

RM, Ohio

Dear RM,

Times they are a-changin', eh, RM? It seems that the time-honored tradition of law school—stamping and sealing hundreds and hundreds of letters addressed to "Hiring Partner"—is a practice facing its golden years.

Ah—but not so fast, RM. The Job Goddess posed your question to a number of legal employers, most of whom feel this way about e-mail: While it is perfectly fine for informal correspondence, like a note to an alum from your school asking for advice about breaking into the legal market in their city, or inviting a friend of a friend out for a cup of coffee to pick their brain about being an entertainment lawyer, it's probably ***too*** informal for your standard, "Dear Attorney Godzilla: Rodan, your colleague, suggested I should contact you because of your expertise in construction law . . . yadda yadda yadda." If you think about the e-mail you yourself get,

RM—and at this point I am not discussing the rather graphic jokes about Bill Gates that seem to make their way into many of the e-mails the Job Goddess receives—you'll note that they tend to fall into the "just a quick question" category. Formal correspondence over the Internet is just a little bit off-putting, at least right now.

The Job Goddess has a sneaking suspicion that the way society is progressing, this won't be a column for the ages. But for right now, RM—if you insist on doing your job search in writing, keep that tongue busy licking those envelopes. But you know what the Job Goddess **really** wants, RM. She wants you to avoid letters altogether, and e-mail a casual note to those friends of friends (or alums), meet them, and through them meet **their** friends—your potential employers—in person. **That's** your best, surest, and fastest way to the job of your dreams, and it avoids writing icky cover letters altogether.

ETERNALLY YOURS,

The Job Goddess

Is It Worth Going to a Headhunter for My First Legal Job?

Dear Job Goddess,

I have been sending out a bunch of letters in hopes of finding a job after graduation, with no success. I have been thinking about trying a different strategy and *using a headhunter. How effective **are** legal placement agencies in finding jobs for recent law school grads? And if they **are** effective, can you recommend any around Philadelphia?*

MF, Pennsylvania

Dear MF,

Things are a lot brighter than they seem right now, MF, even though the Job Goddess has got to start you out with a bit o' bad news: don't waste your time even **contacting** headhunters, not for at least a year. The Job Goddess will elaborate a bit on exactly why this is so, but it basically boils down to this: as a new law school graduate, you don't yet have a head worth being hunted.

Let's take a moment, shall we, MF, and discuss the world of headhunters in the legal market. Our guide will be Sue Gainen, Career Services Director at the University of Minnesota Law School—and herself a headhunter for seven years in a prior incarnation. She explains that "The way headhunters get paid is that when an employer hires you through them, they get a commission of 25 to 30% of your first year's salary." (The Job Goddess hastens to point out that this payment system accounts for that—ahem—not particularly shy and retiring personality headhunters are known to have.) So if you're talking about a job that pays, say, $75,000 to start, the employer is going to have to cough up 25 grand if they hire someone through a headhunter. And what does **that,** in turn, tell you? That "Headhunters are the employer's sources of employees of last resort," as Sue Gainen says. In other words, an employer is really going to need an expert on Iranian freedom of religion issues **right now** before they're going to go to a headhunter to find said person. The Job Goddess acknowledges that that is a rather obvious exaggeration, but you get the point, MF. In order to entice a headhunter, you've "Got to bring expertise to the table," as Sue Gainen points out. Most law firms are **deluged** with resumes of new law school graduates, a flood to which you yourself have contributed, MF. They don't **have** to cough up a five-figure financial hairball to find you. And they don't.

What does this mean to **you**, MF? It means that barring the unusual—for instance, you neglected to mention your U.S. Supreme Court Clerkship, or that your initials aren't really MF but instead JFK, Jr.—most headhunters won't talk to you for your first foray into the legal job market.

But all is most definitely **not** lost, largely because you can be your own headhunter, and you'll be far more effective than anybody could be on your behalf. After all, what a headhunter does is to bring you to the attention of employers, and entice them to hire you. You're far better qualified, and motivated, to entice them yourself. What you have to do is to get yourself in front of potential employers, in the way that you find most comfortable. If it's Philadelphia you want, you can, for example, find out who runs the local bar association section on the specialty you want to enter. Call that person, and in your most enthusiastic tone, volunteer to help out any way you can—be it organizing events, researching issues, whatever—and explain that you're doing this to break into the field, in Philadelphia. Or visit law firms, in person, and drop off your resume, instead of sending it. The Job Goddess has never known **anyone** who required more than a week to find a job when they took this "personal visit" route, because legal employers are so impressed when law school graduates do **anything** to break out of the "mass mailer" mode. There are a bunch of **other** things you can do, MF—most of which are outlined in the Job Goddess's book, *Guerrilla Tactics for Getting the Legal Job of Your Dreams*. But you get the point. Don't waste time contacting headhunters who aren't motivated to help you find that first job. Contact them a couple of years from now, when you've taken the Job Goddess's advice, found that first job yourself, developed an expertise—and **then** watch those headhunters jump through hoops for you. You'll deserve it!

ETERNALLY YOURS,

The Job Goddess

How Do I Handle Job Ads That Want 'One to Three Years of Experience,' if I'm a New Graduate?

DEAR JOB GODDESS,

I am very frustrated. I'm in my last year of law school, and it seems as though all of the ads I see are looking for somebody with one to three years of experience. Is there any way I can get one of these jobs anyway?

VS, Massachusetts

DEAR VS,

There may well be, VS, and the Job Goddess congratulates you for contacting her instead of just throwing in the career towel.

From the outset you have to appreciate that what employers **advertise** for and what they will **accept** are often two very different things. Many employers have pointed out to the Job Goddess that when they write job ads, they are describing their "ideal" candidate. It is often the case, VS, that that ideal candidate may not apply for the job, and so it will go to someone who—like you—does not have the exact credentials stated in the ad.

With that in mind, how do you improve your odds of being the lucky candidate? Lisa Lesage, Career Services Director at Lewis & Clark Law School (and herself an attorney for several years), gives you two steps to follow: one is researching what you've got, and the other is finding out all you can about the employer.

When you look at what you bring to the table, Lisa Lesage says that, "When attorneys say they want one to three years of experience, what they really want is someone who knows the ropes. Jobs you have during law school can easily give you that." She advises you to "Look at all the law-related work you've done, no matter what it is, and disgorge a line or two on every single thing. Don't simply say that you 'researched issues' or 'drafted memoranda and motions.' Instead, be very specific. Say that you drafted a motion for summary judgment in a 1983 case concerning privilege. Or that you prepared a deposition for a Title 7 case involving sexual harassment." For non-legal jobs you've had, be similarly specific so that you can pull out the skills that you can transfer to the legal job you want. Lisa Lesage advises that "If you managed a restaurant before law school, don't just leave it at that. How many people did you manage? Did you handle budgets, or scheduling, or any other activities that would be similar in any setting?" The important thing here is that you "shouldn't ever self-select out!"

What will this self-research do for you, VS? As Lisa Lesage says, "It will help give you fodder for a cover letter, and it will also help you overcome any interview objections. You will be able to say, 'I may have just graduated, but I've got the experience you're looking for.'"

The other task at hand for you, VS, is to research the employer. Most ads state whom the employer is; if you find ads that don't—in other words, it's a "blind ad"—you are not out of luck. Lisa Lesage says that, "If the return address is a P.O. Box, and the employer is incorporated, the post office must tell you the name of the box holder. Once you know who the employer is, go to your career services office at school and see if they've compiled data on the employer or if there are alums from your school who have worked there." Such an alum can be an enormous help, since they will not only be able to tell you about the employer and how you can position yourself to get a job there—but they may also be willing to walk your application over to the person who's doing the hiring, and perhaps even put in a good word for you. Needless to say, this is a great way to distinguish yourself from other people applying for the same job.

Of course, VS, you know that the Job Goddess prefers that you find your dream job by getting to know people, through school and law-related activities, than through job ads. But the fact remains that many people **do** find jobs they like through ads, and if you follow the advice here—why, VS, there's no reason why you can't as well.

ETERNALLY YOURS,

The Job Goddess

What Gives With Mass Mailers?

DEAR JOB GODDESS,

 I read your book "Guerrilla Tactics for Getting the Legal Job of Your Dreams," and I know you are

*really against mass mailers. Don't they **ever** work? If they're such a bad idea, why does everybody do them?*

CF, Pennsylvania

Dear CF,

Moo-oo-oo. That's why, CF. Everybody does them, well, because everybody has **always** done them. It's the equivalent of salmon spawning. And in the Job Goddess's mind, that's simply not a good enough reason to do **anything**.

But does that mean mass mailers never work? Of course not. For one thing, CF, if you've got mind-boggling paper credentials, mass mail away. If your letter begins "As President of the Harvard Law Review, I . . . " you could etch your resume on a rock and hurl it through law firm windows and get job offers.

Of course, that isn't most law students. It certainly wasn't the Job Goddess when she was in law school. And outside of the grade-blessed, the mass mailer statistics are pathetic. As a rule of thumb, only one or two percent of mass-mailed letters result in interviews. So a typical law student can expect one or two thumbs-ups for every hundred letters they mail. While that is abysmal, it contains the essence of why the Job Goddess can't **universally** condemn mass mailers. As Gloria Yolanda Rivera, the Career Services Director at St. John's University School of Law, says, "Four interviews from 200 letters are four interviews you didn't have otherwise. Out of those four, you just might get an offer."

But there's a catch, CF, and it's this: the Job Goddess has yet to find the law student who can easily stomach dozens and dozens of rejections without having their morale beaten into a spiritual pulp. If you go into a mass mailer realizing two important facts, you might be able to overcome this overwhelming rejection and make a mass mailer work for you. One fact is this: those paper rejections are meaningless. The Job Goddess knows a number of law students who were rejected repeatedly by a given employer when that employer was lumped into a mass-mailer—only to subsequently find themselves invited for an interview when they met one of the attorneys in the firm at a job fair, bar meeting, or conference. Same students, same credentials, totally different result. So blame your mass mailer rejections on the approach, not *yourself*.

The other point to remember about mass mailers is the importance of not making them the sole focus of your job search. Because mass mailers take so much time to put together, and are so physically impressive—all of those envelopes! All of those stamps!—you'll be tempted to do nothing else. As Wendy Werner, Career Services Director at the St. Louis University School of Law, comments, "It's so much more comfortable to do a paper search, and have your paper meet their paper." Please don't let that happen to you, CF—if necessary, jettison the mass mailer and do everything else, *anything* else, instead. The happiest law school graduates the Job Goddess knows are those who got their jobs by being flesh and blood human beings—by meeting their prospective employers in person, through school activities, volunteering at legal functions, attending conferences, and the like. Great jobs, all over the world, have fallen into students' laps when they made the effort to be a smiling face instead of a standardized letter. And that, of course, is what—caution: shameless commercial plug ahead—the Job Goddess's fabulous book, *Guerrilla Tactics*, teaches you how to do, no matter how shy you are.

So, yes, CF, mass mailers aren't a *total* loss. But the Job Goddess believes you deserve so much better than that, CF!

ETERNALLY YOURS,

The Job Goddess

Taking Their Eye
Off the Ball

*Getting Employers to Focus on
What You've Got, Instead of What
You Don't Have*

Getting Another Employer to Want You ...
When Your Summer Clerkship Employer Didn't

Dear Job Goddess,

The worst thing that could possibly happen, happened. On the last day of my summer clerkship, the hiring partner called me in. I was sure I was going to get an offer, but instead he said, "I'm afraid we're not going to be inviting you back." I was so shocked that I don't remember anything he said after that. I'm dreading the prospect of interviewing with other firms because I know they'll ask me if I got an offer. Tell me, Job Goddess, what should I say?

MT, Colorado

Dear MT,

The Job Goddess realizes that the last thing you need to hear right now is that annoying business about silver linings, MT. But you need to know that for all the pain you feel right now, many of the happiest law school graduates are those who got the heave-ho after their summer clerkship. To get from here to there, MT, you've got to realize that it really doesn't matter that you didn't get an offer—what counts is how you **present** it to future employers. And in order to make a convincing presentation, you need to do a bit of spadework.

First, you've got to determine **exactly** what happened. The Job Goddess realizes that you're in shock, but you must take a deep breath, and look for clues. As Suzanne Mitchell, Career Services Director at the University of

Chicago Law School advises, "Tell the story of your summer. Look at your assignments and interactions with lawyers at the firm and your reviews, and see if you can piece it together." Were you too proud to ask questions about your assignments, such that you turned in work your supervisors couldn't use? Or was your research incomplete, or your documents misspelled and shoddy-looking? Did you miss deadlines? Did you lock horns with somebody important?

If you honestly cannot figure it out, call the firm and ask why you weren't invited back. Suzanne Mitchell warns you, "Don't be defensive! This is a fact-finding mission. You aren't offering excuses for what happened or defending your work. Instead, you need to say something like, 'I'm not challenging or blaming, but I need to know what to do to succeed.'" Listen carefully to what you are told and see what you might do to avoid having the same problem happen again.

As you do this evaluation, you might find, MT, that the underlying problem was actually that you sabotaged yourself. Ask yourself: Did you really want the job, or did you really not want to be rejected? If you didn't want the job, you may have subconsciously dropped the ball to avoid having to turn down an offer. You wouldn't be alone, MT—studies show that as many as a third of law students don't actually want to be lawyers! And if that's the case for you, your firm did you a favor by encouraging you to determine ***right now***, instead of five years down the road, exactly what it is that you ***do*** want.

Once you've figured out what went wrong, you need to find out from the firm what they are going to say when prospective employers call them. As Suzanne Mitchell says, "Don't assume that people won't call! They ***will***." Seek out people who are willing to say good things about your work, and write down their names, addresses and phone numbers.

Now that you've learned about what went wrong along with what the firm will say, plan what you yourself will say. The key here is to focus on what you *learned* as a result of your non-offer. For instance, if the problem is that you didn't ask questions about your assignments, you can say something like, "Frankly, I was afraid of looking stupid, so that when I got assignments I sometimes researched issues that my supervisors didn't really want to know about. That taught me a valuable lesson about making sure I have my assignments crystal clear. When I *did* clarify my assignments, the lawyers I worked for were very happy with my work. In fact, here are their names and phone numbers—they can tell you about the quality of my work"—at this point, of course, you'd fork over the list of attorneys who'll say nice things about you.

The key here, MT, as Suzanne Mitchell points out, is to "Practice what you'll say, until you feel as comfortable talking about it as you would talking about the weather." Be sure not to answer a monosyllabic "no" when you're asked about whether you got an offer. Remember: It's not the substance of what happened, but rather what it portends for your *future* employers. If you can credibly explain why your summer bugbear will not reappear, you've vanquished the problem.

The Job Goddess knows that you will find it hard to believe that you can overcome a non-offer this easily—but you *can*, MT. In fact, no matter how much it hurts right now, in the long run you really will be much better off. Why is that? As Suzanne Mitchell explains, "A rejection forces you to do something everyone should do, but most people don't: think about what you're really good at, what you really want." So your rejection will unwittingly ensure your happiness in the long run. The Job Goddess can—ahem—attest to this first-hand. She summer-clerked for a mega-firm that told her, at the end of the summer, that, unlike Jesus, she wouldn't be coming back. If not for that rejection, the Job Goddess might never have become the Job Goddess. (Of course, while she is ultimately grateful to that firm for rejecting her, the firm nonetheless does not make an appearance in the Job Goddess's new-and-sure-to-be-a-blockbuster, *America's Greatest Places to Work With a Law Degree.*)

So, MT, follow the steps the Job Goddess has outlined for you—and realize that your unlucky summer does not mark you for life any more than it defined the Job Goddess.

ETERNALLY YOURS,

The Job Goddess

———

Getting Employers to Focus on A-bilities Instead of Visible DIS-abilities

DEAR JOB GODDESS,

 I have a very visible disability, which is made even more prominent by the fact that I am helped by a huge black dog. On top of that, my grades are not what they could be because I was hospitalized the last two weeks of fall term. Some people tell me to tell potential employers that my grades were due to the fact that there was a seven-year gap between college and law school, implying that I am a bit rusty. I feel uncomfortable with this suggestion because it is not the truth and I am a poor liar. How can I encourage potential employers to look past my disability and focus on my skills? And do you have any special strategies or suggestions for job-hunters with disabilities?

MC, Oregon

Dear MC,

Well, yes, as a matter of fact, MC, the Job Goddess *does* have some special strategies for job-hunters with disabilities. Hmmm. And maybe, just maybe, that's how your letter snuck to the top of the Job Goddess's "in-box."

In one important respect, your job search is no different than anybody else's, in the sense that you've got to show potential employers what it is that you bring to the table for them. And in that sense, what you should do is very much similar to what any law student seeking a great job ought to do—put yourself in a position where potential employers get to see what you can do, *outside* of a formal cover letter and job interview. How do you do that? Well, let's assume that you want to practice law in the city where you live now. What you could do is to contact the lawyer in the local bar association who heads the specialty you want to practice. Offer to volunteer on researching an issue, helping out on a project, or planning an event. You could do the same thing for organizations that run continuing legal education seminars in the specialty you want to enter; offer to help out at the next seminar. What you're accomplishing when you do things like this is to say, "See? I'm not just *telling* you what I can do; I'm *showing* you." And you're doing so in a context in which you don't feel the pressure of a job interview, and the people you meet won't feel the direct pressure of a hiring decision. Once they get to know you, and like you, they'll naturally think of you as a potential employee—or recommend you to people who will.

Another alternative is to consider your disability as a means of connecting with people who might help you kick off your career. While you don't mention it per se in your letter, the fact that you travel with a large black dog suggests that you're visually impaired (if the Job Goddess guessed wrong, she apologizes). If so, think about organizations that support the visually impaired. Go to people who run and support those organizations, say that you want to practice law, and ask whom they believe you ought to talk to for advice and leads on getting your career started. Because they know you via your disability, you don't have to worry about how they will react to you—and they will naturally be supportive. You will also want to ask them for anyone they know of who already practices law with your disability. The news media is another good source for stories about lawyers who are similarly disabled. Regardless of how you find out about them, contact those lawyers, explain that you have the same disability they have, and see if they'll informally mentor you. Again, because they can identify with you—and, not for nothing, you're flattering them by holding them up as a role model—they'll be predisposed to help you. Do you notice something ironic here, MC? You are accessing a whole raft of people who would not have a special incentive to help you if you **weren't** disabled.

So much for special strategies. The other part of your letter seems to focus on what you ought to do if you send out letters seeking interviews—the traditional approach to finding a job. Not coincidentally, it is an approach that the Job Goddess eschews, because she believes, disabled or not, that you stand a far greater chance of landing a rewarding job if you get to know people **outside** of a job interview. But, ho hum, let's look at the letter-and-interview scenario. Rob Kaplan, the Associate Dean and Career Services Director at the William & Mary Law School (and a partner in a law firm in a prior life), advises that you "Don't make a special point of mentioning your disability in your letter or resume." Instead, when you get nibbles in the form of phone calls, mention your disability in a casual way—for instance, if you are wheelchair-bound, say so in the context of asking whether the building is wheelchair-accessible. The reason for this? Because most employers, when asked about people with visible disabilities, prefer not to be surprised at the interview. By mentioning your disability up front, you're eliminating that element of surprise.

Then, at the interview itself, Rob Kaplan suggests that you "Take the offensive—it will help you establish a rapport! You might want to say something like, 'In your position, I'd be concerned about my disability and would want to know about it.'" Go on to talk about everything you've done to overcome any obstacles posed by your disability, and how well you will function in spite of it, drawing on examples of prior work (whether in law school or beforehand) to back up what you say. As Rob Kaplan points out, when you take this approach, you're "Putting the interviewer's mind at ease, as well as showing that you're comfortable talking about it."

Finally, regarding the grades issue, the Job Goddess applauds your instincts about not lying. What many innocently misguided job seekers believe—including among them, unfortunately, some people who have advised you—is that getting a great job has to involve deception. It doesn't. Getting a great job means putting the most positive possible spin on the truth. In your case, as Rob Kaplan puts it, this means "Explaining that you had a medical problem that kept you out of school right before exams." As he points out, everybody at some time or another has had to miss time from school because of a medical problem; there's no reason to lie about it. Instead, what you can do is focus on how well you're doing *now*, without a medical absence to hold you back. And if your grades still aren't great, well—time to focus on your strengths by highlighting research you've done for a professor, or skills you bring forward from your prior career, or work you've done for any other legal employer.

The Job Goddess is confident that you see the pattern here, MC—instead of focusing on DIS-abilities, you're focusing on A-bilities. And in doing so, you're doing everything you need to nail down that job you want.

E T E R N A L L Y   Y O U R S ,

The Job Goddess

Should I Tell Interviewers About a Non-Obvious Physical Problem?

Dear Job Goddess,

I am a 2L. I am getting ready to go on some job interviews, and I don't know whether I should mention in interviews that I suffer from narcolepsy. If you think I **should** mention it, what should I say so that I don't alienate potential employers?

PL, Minnesota

Dear PL,

You'd be surprised how many people approach the Job Goddess with your predicament, PL—not narcolepsy, exactly, but with a whole variety of non-obvious problems and ailments, from recovering cancer victims to epileptics to people with non-physical problems, like foreigners with visa issues. Sigh. You name it,

PL, the Job Goddess has heard it. The question of when—and if—to "come clean" justifiably produces a lot of anxiety. The Job Goddess has consulted with many employers and career counselors about this issue, and the consensus is this—if the problem/ailment will impact your work, you have an obligation to tell (and the Job Goddess will help you with the presentation in just a minute). If it *won't*, then you can keep it to yourself with the Job Goddess's blessing.

When the Job Goddess talks about "impacting your work," PL, there are two likely categories: finances and performance. Sometimes people have a pre-existing medical condition that will affect their employer's insurance rates. While the Job Goddess doubts narcolepsy fits this description, calling your state's labor or insurance department would give you the definitive answer to this question without you having to question the employer directly (and the employer might not know the answer to this, anyway). And while the Job Goddess is not addressing issues of whether the ADA (Americans With Disabilities Act) would demand that an employer ignore the issue, everyone the Job Goddess consulted—employers and career counselors—agreed that you ought to let employers know about it.

This, by the way, would cover another set of problems that are non-medical—namely, visa problems. The Job Goddess knows many foreign law students who accept job offers knowing that their employers will have to foot a substantial visa-related bill in hiring them. The Job Goddess believes that the Golden Rule is best followed in circumstances like these.

The other possible impact on your work that would demand disclosure relates to performance. As a narcoleptic, if you are likely to fall asleep at any moment during the day, this would impact some kinds of legal work more than others. For instance, working in a research capacity, for an appellate judge or at a large firm, for instance, wouldn't be greatly affected by your narcolepsy—whereas working as a public defender, assistant state's attorney, or in any capacity where sudden bouts of narcolepsy would be more remarkable, would require disclosure. Even clerking for a trial-level judge might demand that you say something ahead of time, *especially* if the judge would expect you, for instance, to drive him/her from location to location.

If your condition *does* auger for disclosure for either of these reasons, PL, the Job Goddess understands from her experts that this is how you ought to accomplish it so that it doesn't tank your job chances. First of all, plan, and *practice*, the words you will use to explain your condition. Say them over and over until you can talk about it without flinching, apologizing, or seeming uncomfortable. A quietly confident matter-of-factness is the tone you should aim for. Say something like, "Talking to you about what you do has made me even *more* excited to join you than I was before. But I need to tell you about something you should know about me, and to explain it to you. I have narcolepsy. And while it doesn't affect me most of the time, I occasionally suddenly fall asleep for about 30 seconds (or whatever the actual statistics are, PL). It typically happens about three times a week. I'm happy to answer any questions you have about it, but I want to assure you up front that I've researched the kind of work you'd expect me to do, and I wouldn't be here, wasting your time, if I wasn't confident I could do everything you ask of me. If anything, overcoming this problem has made me even more determined to prove I can do a great job for you." Such candor will not only earn you respect, but your calm explanation of it will engender confidence in you, PL—which is exactly what you want to achieve in *any* job interview.

If, on the other hand, your affliction will *not* impact your employer, you don't have an obligation to say *anything* about it. As the Job Goddess often counsels, interviews are for jobs—they aren't confessionals. However, the Job Goddess is sensitive to the fact that you may *want* to disclose your affliction to your potential employer. You may feel more comfortable with them knowing about it. In that case, after you have accepted an offer, tell your employer about it, stating that it makes you more comfortable for them to know about it up front, not because it will affect your work—it won't, otherwise you would have told them about it before they made you an offer.

So there you have it, PL. The Job Goddess has seen many extraordinary law students overcome all *kinds* of obstacles and go on to brilliant careers. She's confident you can—and will—do the same.

ETERNALLY YOURS,

The Job Goddess

Turning Two Dimensions Into Three

Resumes

I Used to Be a Hooters Girl.
Should I Put It on My Resume?

Dear Job Goddess,

I don't know whether I should put my work experience prior to law school on my resume. I was a Hooters girl. I probably wouldn't even ask except that I have a friend at law school who used to be a male stripper, and it doesn't seem to hurt him. What do you think?

DK, California

Dear DK,

The Job Goddess thinks, DK, that this is one situation where you don't want to make a clean breast of things. (The Job Goddess apologizes, DK, but she couldn't resist.)

The most important thing to realize is that in the long run, your hooting experience won't hurt you one bit. The Job Goddess has been positively startled to find out, in fact, that many respected members of the legal profession got their start in various states of undress; why, there is a federal judge in the Northeast who used to be a Playboy bunny. The question is, DK, how do you get from here to there?

The problem is, of course, that the moment you mention to anyone that you've been a Hooters girl, well, that's what they're going to remember about you. As Susan Gainen, Career Services Director at the University of Minnesota School of Law, explains, "Sure, there are some people who will think it's amusing. But others are going to believe you're a traitor to your gender. And still others won't take you seriously if they meet you knowing that you were a Hooters girl."

So, what should you do? "Simply put 'other experience' on your resume, list 'Waitressed,' and put Hooters, corporate name, if it doesn't give away the fact that it was Hooters. A lot of restaurants are owned by parent companies that go by an entirely different name. Regardless of whether you include the corporate name or not, put down how many hours a week you worked, and how much of your education you financed as a result," says Susan Gainen. By doing so, you will focus on your work ethic, and that's a huge positive. Why, the Job Goddess knows a law student who worked her way through law school at a nightclub, serving Jell-o shots on Friday and Saturday nights. She pulled in over $1,000 a weekend this way, and got out of law school debt-free. Leading one, perhaps naturally, to question, "Why not keep the Jell-o shots job and chuck law school?" Ah, but the letters "Esq." look so much more impressive on one's business card than "Semi-molten beverage purveyor."

Do not take any of this to suggest that being a Hooters girl is something to be embarrassed about, DK. The point is that, as Sue Gainen explains, "Law school is one of those times in life when you can reinvent yourself. You don't lie about your past, but you can shade and shadow what you've done if you no longer want to be known that way." To be perfectly blunt, DK, you now want to be known as the smartest, most personable, most insightful lawyer you can be. You don't want lawyers on the hiring committee to say, when your name comes up, "Oh, yeah, her. Nice rack."

Once they know you, DK, everything changes. Most people will think it's cool that you were a Hooters girl. Frankly, the Job Goddess thinks it's, well, a hoot. But nonetheless, until you have your dream job, the least-risk alternative is to speak of your experience in general terms.

If someone in an interview pins you to specifics, fine; as Sue Gainen says, "At least you'll have shown that you're discreet." Just tell them where you worked, but add that the reason you didn't say that on your resume is that you don't want to be prejudged. After all, you got out of your experience what every waitperson does, no matter where they work—namely, great skills working with people.

As for your male stripper colleague . . . well, DK, as Sue Gainen says, "It's funny, it's not fair, but it's true—he won't be misjudged, but you will." It's a man's world, DK, at least when it comes to jobs that require varying states of dishabille.

By the way, DK, when you have followed the Job Goddess's advice and scaled the heights in your legal career, may the Job Goddess propose a title for your memoirs? "From Hooters to the Supreme Court."

The Job Goddess thanks you for letting her get that off her chest.

ETERNALLY YOURS,

The Job Goddess

Business Card Resumes: Good Idea, or Boner?

DEAR JOB GODDESS,

 One of my friends showed me something called a "business card resume." What he did was to have these business cards printed up, with his name and phone *number on one side, and highlights from his resume on the other side. He said a bunch of people are doing this, so that when they meet potential employers they hand over these cards. Should I bother getting some for myself?*

Curious in Chicago

Dear Curious,

Sigh. You know, Curious, that the Job Goddess takes a fairly dim view of resumes as a job-finding tool, even in their full-blown, bond-papered, engraved 8 ½" x 11" incarnation. And here you ask her about a business card resume, two steps further down the resume food chain. So, no, you *shouldn't* bother with business card resumes. Here's why.

Think for a moment, Curious, about the kind of circumstance in which you'd be tempted to whip out one of these incredible shrinking resumes. You're at a social gathering. You happen to meet Will Winken, of the law firm Winken, Blinken, and Nod, and it becomes clear fairly quickly that Will is (i) friendly, and (ii) a potential employer. The surest way to turn this chance encounter into a job is to use it as the basis for future contact. As Carolyn Bregman, Career Services Director at Emory Law School, points out, "Follow up with a phone call or note, mentioning something Winken said to you." You can say that you'd like to learn more about whatever it is he said, or that you've since read more about him and found that he's an expert on phlegm reclamation law and how that's a topic that's always fascinated you; invite him for coffee at his convenience so you can learn more about it. What have you done? *You've taken a social encounter and turned it into a potential job opportunity.* And that makes the Job Goddess very proud.

But what happens if you, instead, whip out your business card resume, and say, "Gee, Mr. Winken, nice meeting you. Here's my business card resume, in case you ever need anybody like me." *Now* what have you done? You have, with one simple gesture, wiped out any excuse to follow up! Instead of having a phone call or a note from you that is personalized to Winken, you've got a piddling little standardized card with your vital statistics on it. Ugh. Curious, I know you're much more memorable than anything you could possibly fit on the back of a business card.

So there you have it, Curious. Save the money you'll spend on a business card resume, and spend it later, when you have a ***real*** business card to print, reading, "Curious, Esq.; Winken, Blinken, and Nod; Attorneys at Law."

ETERNALLY YOURS,

The Job Goddess

Handling Jekyll & Hyde Grades

DEAR JOB GODDESS,

I just started my second year in law school, and I don't know what to do about my grades on my resume. My first semester grades were terrible and my second semester I did much better. Overall I am in the middle of my class. What should I put on my resume? Is it possible to highlight my second semester performance and hide what happened before?

NR, North Carolina

Dear NR,

For all practical purposes, yes, you *can* hide your slow start. The Job Goddess doesn't mean to suggest that you actually, physically ditch your overall GPA or your unfortunate first semester, NR. But you *can* take advantage of the psychology of resume readers to make your first semester *seem* invisible.

How? As Kathy Brady, Career Services Director at Fordham Law School, explains, "You have to realize that most people just scan resumes, from top to bottom and left to right. The first number they see on the left-hand side of the page is the one they'll remember."

With that in mind, NR, you need to take your three figures—your second semester average, your first semester average, and your overall GPA—and space them out on your resume with the best grades flush left, the worst semester in the middle, and your overall GPA flush right, like this:

Second Semester GPA   First Semester GPA   Overall GPA

With the natural way people scan a page, the first number your readers will see, and the only one they're likely to remember, is that second semester GPA. And whaddya know—that's *exactly* what you want them to do.

Incidentally, NR, your law school colleagues who are metaphysically peering over your shoulder and reading this advice will enjoy knowing that this spatial set-up can cure a variety of credential ailments. It obviously would work if you were a third year, and had one year of law school when your grades far surpassed those of your other year.

It would also work in a situation where you excelled in classes relevant to the employer, and not in others. For instance, let's say that you wanted to work for the prosecutor's office, where your wonderful grades in classes like Criminal Law, Criminal Procedure, Trial Tactics, and Research and Writing would be most relevant. You'd set up your 'grades' line as follows:

GPA in relevant classes	GPA in other classes	Overall GPA

"Well, OK, Job Goddess," she hears you saying. "What if your grades don't divide so nicely into positives and negatives?" The Job Goddess reminds you that mediocre grades do not a mediocre lawyer make, as the Job Goddess has advised in previous columns and will undoubtedly revisit in the future. To put it briefly, employers don't care about what you *can't* do for them, but what you *can*. When you prove that to their satisfaction—whether in the form of grades, or work experience, or volunteer positions, or anything else—you'll get the offer.

ETERNALLY YOURS,

The Job Goddess

Should I Put Hobbies and Interests on My Resume?

DEAR JOB GODDESS,

 Should I put hobbies on my resume? Some people say yes, others say no. What do you think? And if you think I should, what kinds of hobbies look good?

TR, Georgia

Dear TR,

The Job Goddess is frightfully curious as to exactly what your hobbies *are*, TR, that you would be concerned about whether they 'look good'— but perhaps she is still reacting to the "Hooters girl" letter she received a couple of months ago.

The Job Goddess has often fielded questions like yours, TR, and that has given her the opportunity to get feedback from many experts about the hobby issue. In general, employers do prefer to see hobbies and interests on resumes, but as Beth Kirch, Career Services Director at the University of Georgia Law School points out, "Don't put just any hobby or interest. If they're something like 'reading' or 'jogging,' that is unlikely to help you most of the time. If it's something interesting or it shows leadership, then it will help you."

Beyond that, TR, be on the lookout for hobbies or interests that exhibit other traits the Job Goddess has heard about: hobbies or interests that show discipline, or rainmaking ability, or a connection with the employer.

Let's see how these hobbies work, in practice. There is a universe of interesting hobbies. The Job Goddess knows of one law student who wowed an on-campus interviewer by mentioning on his resume that he could do perfect imitations of both Elvises, Costello and Presley. The interviewer noticed this immediately and said, "Is it true?" When the student said that it was, the interviewer said, "Well, let's see them!" The student proceeded to do flawless imitations of the Elvises, and was rewarded with a callback interview.

Of course, hobbies don't have to be *that* interesting to generate enthusiasm! For instance, jogging might not flip anybody's switch, whereas taking part in mini-triathlons would—it's both interesting and it takes an awful lot of discipline, at least more than the bon-bon eating Job Goddess has. Golf or tennis, on the other hand, isn't terribly interesting or exotic, but many new associates have told the Job Goddess that if there was one thing they could have changed about law school, they would have taken the time to learn how to play golf. (It can be that integral to—ahem—client development.) And any hobby or interest is elevated to the level of "must-appear-on-resume" if you know, ahead of time, that the interviewer, or everyone at the office, takes part in a certain hobby—fly fishing, or softball, or basketball, for instance. Especially at smaller law firms, there is often an extracurricular activity that bonds the lawyers together—and if you find out what that activity is and it appears on your resume, you've got a clear advantage over those who did not unearth that tidbit of law firm culture.

Having said all of this, the Job Goddess has some very serious words of caution for you. First, and most importantly, don't lie. Don't even exaggerate. If you think there is very little possibility your fib will ever be exposed, the Job Goddess assures you that it happens all the time, and being caught in a lie will put your head in the job search guillotine on the spot. Needless to say, some of the Job Goddess's favourite job search stories involve this very issue. In her *Guerrilla Tactics for Getting the Legal Job of Your Dreams*, she recounts the story of the student who put "golf" as a hobby on his resume. An employer called to interview him, saying that since they both played golf, the interview ought to take place over a game at the employer's country club. Of course, the student couldn't really play golf; when he put "golf" on his resume, he meant that he liked to watch it on TV. The Job Goddess leaves it to your imagination, TR, to envision the upshot of this interview.

Another student, feeling stating an interest in classical music was a bit too mundane, put on his resume that he was interested in seventeenth-century Viennese opera. At one interview, the employer noticed this and said eagerly, "You, too? Which is your favorite?" (The student responded, perfectly honestly when you think about it, "Gee, it's so hard to choose.") Another student stated on his resume that his hobby was "Japanese animation," leading one to believe that he liked to create cartoons. No; what he meant was that he liked to watch "Speed Racer." Yet another student stated that he liked to read novels in Flemish. It just so happened that at one firm where he interviewed—a firm with an international practice—one of the lawyers had just received a piece of correspondence, in Flemish, and figured that since this student knew how to speak Flemish there was no point in having the letter professionally translated. Except that when the lawyer handed the student the letter . . . well, the jig was up.

Clearly you get the Job Goddess's point—don't lie! The other point to remember about hobbies and interests is more subtle, but equally important, and it's this: be aware of the implications of certain hobbies. Most obvious in this regard are partisan politics. Although party politics shows great civic involvement and rainmaking ability, here's the potential problem: if you are heavily involved in one party, lawyers who are equally enamored of the *other* party might fear that you'll bring your politics to the office with you, and an otherwise calm office environment will dissolve into philosophical arguments. For interests like these, the Job Goddess has heard from many people that it is far wiser to research employers before you send them a resume in the first place, to ensure that an important element of your life is shared by those you work with. In fact, the very people you meet in political activities can be excellent dooropeners for you.

But beyond obvious political issues, there is a whole flock of hobbies that are, well, not mainstream. For instance, the Job Goddess herself has long been a Star Trek fan, but she realizes that were this fact to appear on a resume, it would raise the spectre of a fanatic who wears a Star Trek uniform, spends every free moment engaging in role-playing games, and lives for conventions where she might cadge Mr. Sulu's autograph. As a result, putting 'Trekkie' on her resume might not engage employers as she would otherwise hope.

Please, please, please remember, TR, that none of this is engraved in stone. While most lawyers like to see hobbies and interests on a resume, some feel they are out of place. And for every hobby that would leave most lawyers cold, *somebody* will latch onto it immediately. Take synchronized swimming. One student who ignored the advice of her career services director to leave it off her resume, got an interview—and subsequently, a plum job—because one partner who read her resume happened to have a wife who was a synchronized swimmer herself. And another student who actually did put 'Trekkie' on her resume as a hobby landed an interview with a Kentucky firm because they represented a Star Trek cast member in horse disputes. While both of these connections might have been unearthed with an extraordinary amount of research, they were serendipitous. And no amount of good advice, even from the Job Goddess's wonderful experts, can ever make up for that!

So you've got your marching orders, TR. Include those hobbies, as long as they're either interesting, show discipline, rainmaking ability, leadership ability, or make a connection with the employer. And whatever you do, don't lie—it's not just good for your soul, it's good for your job search, too.

ETERNALLY YOURS,

The Job Goddess

Yipes! How to Handle Accuracy-Challenged Resumes That Have Already Reached Employers

Dear Job Goddess,

I did something really stupid, and I need your help. I was a visiting student at a law school that didn't have a traditional grading system. This posed a real problem in trying to convey to law firms exactly how I had done. So I asked the registrar of the school I visited for advice, and she gave me a formula for converting my performance to a traditional 4-point grading system. The formula was complicated, but I finally figured out that I had a 3.7 average, and I put that on my resume and sent it out to law firms. However, after I mailed out my resume, I went back to check my work and realized that I had miscalculated my grades, and that I really only had a 3.46 average. I'm horrified and I have no idea what to do.

LJ, Ohio

Dear LJ,

You know, LJ, the Job Goddess is not proud to admit her first reaction to your letter, which was, "Ha! Like I'm gonna make a Job Goddess column out of *this* one!" For one thing, how often is something like this going to happen to anyone among the minions who read the Goddess?

But then the Goddess mused, and realized that there's a much bigger issue here, one that everybody can identify with. Namely: What do you do when you've sent out correspondence with a big, bad boner in it? People send out accuracy-challenged correspondence all the time. In fact, the Goddess recounts many like stories in her best-seller, *Guerrilla Tactics for Getting the Legal Job of Your Dreams*. There was the one about the young woman who sent out a 300-piece mass mailer, only to find thereafter that on the "objective" line at the top of her resume, she had intended to state, "Seeking a position in public interest." Unfortunately, her spell-checker had over-looked the fact that she dropped the "L" from "public interest." (Think about it for a minute.) And there's another story about a student who sent out a mailer where the letter suggested that he was a first year, but his resume showed him to be a third-year student. What he did was to send out a letter to all of the same people who'd gotten the mailer, stating, "On further review, I find that I am a third-year student."

Stopped cringing yet? OK, LJ, here's what the Goddess's pool of experts had to say about your problem. For a start, it's important to recognize the implication here. If you screwed up your math with *this* formula, what about your accuracy in other matters, like, oh, say, calculating your client's damages? Attention to detail is a crucial skill for lawyers, and that's really what's at stake—not whether your GPA is in actuality a bit lower than your resume states.

But take heart, LJ, because no expert the Goddess con-tacted felt your problem was insurmountable. Here's what to do. First of all, you need to come clean at **some** point, because the truly important fact here is that you didn't mean to deceive anyone; you made an honest com-putation mistake, which is far less serious than any con-scious deception. It's just a matter of figuring out when, and how, to make a clean breast of things. Kathleen Brady, Career Services Director at Fordham University School of Law, suggests that you start by contacting the registrar of the school you visited to find out if other people have made similar mistakes. If the formula is so complicated that many people screw it up, your own boo-boo diminishes in gravity.

Then, you have a choice. One thing you can do is to contact everyone you sent your resume to (you don't state in your letter how many people we're talking about here) and notify them that you accidentally misstated your GPA, state the formula so they can see for themselves how complicated it is and that you've never made a mistake like this (assuming this is true), and explain your obvious mortification. And, as Kathleen Brady suggests, "It wouldn't hurt to make a self-deprecating joke about it. After all, you've got one fact on your side: a lot of people go to law school in the first place because they hate math." Susan Richey, Assistant Dean for Career Services at Franklin Pierce Law School, advocates the idea of contacting everyone who got your resume to notify them of the mistake, because "You never know where you resume will wind up; you don't know who the people you sent it to might pass it along to."

Kathleen Brady says another possibility is to wait and see who's interested in interviewing you, and when they contact you, bring up the mistake and ascertain if they're still interested in interviewing you. As Neal Fillmore, assistant career services director at Franklin Pierce, points out, "After all, we're not talking about a **big** mistake here. A 3.46 instead of a 3.7 is not that big a deal." So, LJ, you've got your marching orders. Come clean, stress that you're not the kind of person who typically makes this kind of mistake, and say something light-hearted about it to cut the tension. Will **everybody** let you off the hook? Maybe not, but at least **some** of them undoubtedly will.

The Job Goddess isn't one to lecture, LJ, but your problem also highlights something else—and that is the importance of finding your dream job by getting to know people instead of sending them letters. If you had, say, met these same potential employers by volunteering on a local bar association committee with them, and then shown them your resume only after they'd stated an interest in hiring you, a mistake like this would hardly show up on the radar screen, because they'd already know—and like—you, as a complete package. The Job Goddess encourages you to get out there and let people get to know *you*, LJ, instead of letting yourself be judged by a crummy piece of paper!

ETERNALLY YOURS,

The Job Goddess

Contact!

Interviews

I Power-Booted A Major Interview. Now What?

Dear Job Goddess,

*I feel like a complete idiot. I went to a job fair and I got an interview with my dream employer. It was scheduled for four o'clock. I didn't want to stand around for the rest of the day so I signed up for three interviews with other employers before that, and they turned out to be all in a row. By the time I got to the interview I really wanted, I was spent. I don't know how to explain what happened except that it was like a nervous breakdown. I couldn't talk at all. I was hyperventilating and everything. The interviewer was really nice and tried to help me calm down but nothing worked. So for the whole 20 minutes I didn't say **anything**. I couldn't pull myself together. This is an employer I really want. What should I do?*

Totally Panicked,

DC, New York

Dear DC,

The Job Goddess has heard many interview disasters, DC, but she must admit that yours is—well—unique. But what it *does* have in common with every other interview disaster that has ever crossed the Job Goddess's heavenly radar screen is this: you *will* overcome it, one way or another.

One option depends on your chutzpah quotient, DC. St. John's University School of Law's Jim Castro-Blanco suggests calling the interviewer, and saying brightly, "Well, you've seen me at my worst. I'd love the chance to let you see me at my best." The interviewer may well admire your courage enough to give you a second chance, and there's no downside risk. Of course, it's possible the interviewer may laugh derisively and say, "Ha! Are you **kidding**?" And, of course, that's where the necessity for chutzpah on your part comes in.

Another lower-chutzpah possibility is to shake the trees for other routes into the same employer. But before you do this, it is vital for you to come up with a credible explanation for your imploding interview, and—most importantly—your explanation must be one that will not reflect on your ability to do the job. For instance, if you are seeking a prosecutor's job, it would not serve you well to explain that, "Oh, I crack under pressure." You'd want to accentuate the fact that this has never happened to you before (the Job Goddess trusts that it hasn't), it won't happen again, and if you can, come up with a quip to lighten the moment—"If Guinness had a record for Most Embarrassing Moments, I think that interview would qualify!"

With your explanation in hand, check with your career services office, your classmates, alumni relations director, professors, alums—anyone you know in the community. Explain your plight and ask for advice. While you might feel bad about your abortive first interview right now, the Job Goddess is hunching that if your approach is smooth enough, your willingness to try again will be viewed as a very positive stick-to-it-iveness.

Of course, DC, it may well be that neither direct nor indirect routes into this particular employer will work—right now. But the Job Goddess need scarcely point out that "right now" isn't terribly meaningful if this really is a dream employer. You've got many decades in front of you, and there's no reason in the world that that dream employer can't be part of your future. By way of analogy the Job Goddess reminds you of the pundits who wrote Richard Nixon's political obituary after his loss in the 1962 California gubernatorial race, when he sneered at the press, "You won't have Dick Nixon to kick around anymore." Remember, it was only six years later that he was elected President. (At which point he gave the press *plenty* of chances to kick him around.)

The message? At worst, think about other things you want to do. It may well be that those alternatives will provide the experience you need to lateral into your dream employer a couple of years down the road. That "apprenticeship" will go far more quickly than you realize right now, DC. And more importantly, the Job Goddess assures you that there are *many* employers for whom you would enjoy working—just as much, if not more, than the one you have in mind right now.

ETERNALLY YOURS,

The Job Goddess

How Do I Handle A Blabby Interviewer?

DEAR JOB GODDESS,

I just had a very weird experience in an interview. I read the stuff in your Guerrilla Tactics book about interviewing, and I was totally prepared, with all of my answers and questions and everything. But it turns out that I didn't get a chance to get a word in edgewise. The interviewer spent the whole time talking about the firm. And what made it even worse was that it was everything I already knew from researching them.

*I feel like the whole interview went by without me get-
ting a chance to sell myself. What should I have done? And
what should I do if it happens again, God forbid?*

KF, Los Angeles

Dear KF,

The Job Goddess's mind boggles at the ways in
which interviewers can surprise us. In her travels,
the Job Goddess has heard everything. Interviewers who
sat silently for 10 minutes, and then calmly reached into
their jacket pocket, took out a pair of scissors, and
snipped the interviewee's tie in half. Interviewers with
bathrooms adjoining their offices, who choose to relieve
themselves during the interview—without closing the
bathroom door. Interviewers who bring a pumpkin and
a knife to an interview, and whose only statement to the
interviewee is, "Carve the pumpkin."

While your experience isn't quite so extreme, KF, it
does fit the mold of the non-interview interview. Of
course, when the interviewer talks about the employer
throughout the interview, there are three likely reasons.
First, your paper credentials are so good that it's a fore-
gone conclusion that they're going to invite you back,
and so they want to sell themselves to you. Second,
your paper credentials are real bow-wows, and so the
interviewer is just going through the motions interviewing you. Or third, the interviewer doesn't know
any better. No matter what the reason, it always makes
sense to try and sneak in a word, and here's how:
Nobody—not even the Job Goddess—can talk for 20
minutes without taking a breath. At the first opportunity, let the interviewer know that you've done your
research about them, and ***immediately*** follow up with a
question to break their flow. For example: "You know, I
read about that merger on your web site. And while I
was there, I looked up your profile and saw that you

wrote a Law Review note about the admissibility of lie detector tests. That's such an interesting topic. How did you choose it?"

Of course, the Job Goddess isn't giving you the precise words to use, KF, but rather pointing out the importance of getting the interviewer away from a prepared script, and into focusing on *this* interview. Look at it this way: If they're already sold on you, this won't un-sell you. And if they've already written you off, showing them your impeccable pre-interview research skills indicates an enthusiasm that fires up many an employer. And if they just don't know any better—well, you've done the interviewer a favor by getting the interview on-track.

There's another option for the blabby interviewer, and it's this: toward the end of the interview, you can say that while you've found the interview fascinating, you wish you'd had a chance to ask some questions of your own—and could you call the interviewer subsequently? This keeps open a valuable line of communication, and very few interviewers will respond with a "No."

Your experience, KF, reminds us all of something very important: it's a mistake to assume that interviewers will be skillful. Virtually no one outside of human resources personnel is trained in interview techniques. And that means that there's a lot of room for you, as the interviewee, to turn the interview into a helpful give-and-take.

ETERNALLY YOURS,

The Job Goddess

How Do I Overcome Being "Interview-Challenged"?

Dear Job Goddess,

I have a self-analysis problem. I am a second-year law student, and I have done well in school. I'm in the top 5% of my class and I'm on Law Review. During on-campus interview season, many firms were anxious to interview me. However, following the interviews, I received very few callbacks and no offers.

I am not socially retarded or anything like that, but I just can't figure out what's going wrong during the interviews. I have heard all of the standard advice about interviewing, and have tried to apply the suggestions. I hate the thought of blowing job prospects just because I am an inept interviewee. Do you have any suggestions?

HB, New York

Dear HB,

The Job Goddess *always* has suggestions— although in your case, HB, she is not entirely proud to admit that one of the reasons she graced your letter with a column is to show your less academically-blessed law school colleagues that great grades and Law Review ain't, to put it in the vernacular, everything. They don't hurt, but as you have so frankly and self-effacingly pointed out, credentials might make it easy to get in the door, but the interview is what seals the deal.

So, what's going on here? Of course without meeting you herself the Job Goddess can't be sure. But having met and spoken with many thousands of law students, HB, she is confident that whatever obstacle you face in interviewing is easily overcome—even though whatever this glitch is may not be obvious to you. The important point to remember about interviewing is that the interviewer doesn't **know** you—they only know what you *present.* An interviewing problem is just a presentation problem. It's a matter of making sure the best "*you*" is the one that comes across.

Three of the more obvious cases the Job Goddess has met immediately come to mind. One charming young man accosted the Job Goddess after one of her *Guerrilla Tactics* seminars, and said, "I do everything you tell us to do. I'm prepared, I have answers ready, I ask lots of questions. I don't know what's wrong." Upon further interrogation, the Job Goddess was horrified to discover that the question he always led with in interviews was, "When's the last time your firm had a group hug?"—apparently as a means of trying to determine the firm's atmosphere. Needless to say, when the Job Goddess gently redirected him away from asking this particular question, the flow of offers quickly began.

Another young man similarly bemoaned an interviewing problem. As the Job Goddess spoke with him, taking a cue from his facial expression, she tried to discern a nasty odor in the air. There was none; this young man's problem was, in fact, that his natural expression was one of mild distaste. He was completely unaware of it until the Job Goddess led him to a mirror and pointed it out.

Finally, the Job Goddess thinks of a young woman who was turning down an offer from her current employer, and believed this was tripping her up in interviews, even though she had an answer fully prepared for questions about it. Unfortunately, when asked why she wasn't staying put, she said, "My employers are completely unorganized. They never get anything accomplished, and it's very frustrating to me." Even though this was the truth, it was the *unvarnished* truth. As the Job Goddess pointed out to her, virtually any interviewer will be able to think of someone in their own office who is unorganized, and the interviewer will extrapolate from her response that this person, too, would drive her crazy, and thus she wouldn't be a good hire. By simply rewording her response, and pointing out how she'd learned to cope with disorganized bosses and was now ready for a different challenge, she corrected this simple—but important—interviewing flaw.

Now, HB, could your problem be a facial expression? An inappropriate question? A poorly worded, albeit truthful, answer? Or perhaps you come across as shy or, God forbid, arrogant in an interview, even though the Job Goddess knows that you are, in your heart, both confident and humble? (The Job Goddess is fairly sure you haven't offended the arrogance gods, HB, since you characterize your perfectly stellar credentials as merely showing that you have "done well.") The best, fastest, and easiest way to cut to the chase is to go to your career services office and request a mock interview, or perhaps a series of them, with different interviewers. If your school has such facilities, request that the interview be videotaped. And prepare for these mock interviews as you would for any interview; tell your career services office what kind of jobs you are seeking, so that they will question you accordingly. How do you prepare? The simplest way is to go to your career services office, library, or your local bookstore, and check out *Guerrilla Tactics for Getting the Legal Job of Your Dreams,* the Job Goddess's much-heralded (at least by the Job Goddess) job search book for law students. It's got an extensive chapter on interviewing. For a start—there's a lot more to it than this, of course, which is why it takes a whole chapter to explain—what you've got to do is learn as much as you can about the employer beforehand, ask lots of questions based on your research and inquire into the interviewer's own experience at the firm, memorize a brief "infomercial" about yourself (to be used for a question like "Tell me about yourself"), and prepare answers, actually **rehearse** them, for any difficult question you might face (the chapter takes you through dozens and dozens of potential questions, as well as great and terrible answers).

When you request such mock interviews, be sure that you lay yourself as bare as you did for the Job Goddess. Say that you know you're doing something wrong, and you sincerely want to find out what it is. That way, you are predisposing your career services director (or whoever conducts your mock interview) to criticize you, which is what you've got to do. Better to have criticism come in the form of helpful hints from a mock interview, than as a rejection from a *real* interview.

If, for some ungodly reason, your career services office doesn't perform mock interviews—and the Job Goddess has never seen such a thing—go to another law school in the area, or a local college, and explain your plight. They will either oblige you, if they feel like being helpful that way, or direct you to a local independent career counselor who will do the same thing.

HB, the Job Goddess is certain that taking these simple steps is all you'll need to do to "lick" your interview problem—and bask in the warm glow of those fabulous credentials!

ETERNALLY YOURS,

The Job Goddess

How to Talk About Class Standing When You're Standing in the Bottom Half of the Class

Dear Job Goddess,

OK, you say not to worry about grades, so I'm not worried. But what do you do when an employer asks you to include your grades on your resume? Do you omit that little part of your life, as if to say, "Oops, overlooked that one"? Or do you tell them that you're in the bottom half of the class? How do you say it tactfully? I've got enough interest, enthusiasm, and experience, but I don't know how and where to address the class standing issue. Help me, Job Goddess!

MF, Oregon

Dear MF,

Sigh. Law school is just awful that way. We come to school with such varied talents and backgrounds, and within one pathetic semester, we are reduced to a GPA tattooed on the inside of our eyelids. Or so we think, eh, MF?

In fact, the Job Goddess encourages you to cheer up, because your grades are not the death sentence you think they are. The Job Goddess *could* take the easy way out, mind you, MF, and direct you to the chapter in her book, *Guerrilla Tactics for Getting the Legal Job of Your Dreams*, which has the catchy title, "Help! My Grades Stink!" But she won't sink that low, and instead will explain to you how you can overcome your grades both in the way you think about them, and the way you present them. (The Job Goddess is confident you will read her book anyway.)

Let's address that thinking part first, MF. It is much too easy to fall victim in law school to the idea that if you aren't graced with grades in the top 10% and are not welcomed onto Law Review, then you—well, you ain't spit. In fact, you can get virtually any job you want regardless of your grades. For some of them, true, you'll have to do something else first to prove that your competence isn't measured by your GPA. But as Susan Gainen, Career Services Director at the University of Minnesota School of Law, points out, "There are only three jobs from the outset that require really high grades, and they are tenure-track law professor, large law firm, and certain judicial clerkships." For everybody else, as Mary Brennan Stich, Associate Dean and Director of Career Services at St. Mary's University School of Law, explains, "Law students don't want to believe it, but most lawyers don't discriminate against people with bad grades. Generally, the ones who *do* were at the top of the class themselves. But most lawyers *weren't* at the top of their class, and they don't expect you to be, either."

What does that tell you, MF? Unless you want to be forced to market yourself aggressively, avoid employers who are going to demand great grades right out of the chute. (As the Job Goddess explains in *Guerrilla Tactics,* if you're going to go after jobs for which you don't have the grades, you can still make it. But it'll demand a lot out of you in terms of effort and tenacity, and it requires more strategy than we've got the room to discuss here.) Instead, market yourself to the rest of the market—and face it, MF, there are many more employers who *don't* have a grade prejudice than who *do.*

And for those employers you *do* go after, keep focused on what that grade issue is all about. It's not about a little smelly number, MF. It's about competence.

Are you competent? Of course you are! So when you are asked about your grades, don't dwell on the one thing—your GPA—that suggests you *aren't!* As Mary Brennan Stich advises, "Don't be defensive! Provide your grades, and then get off it." And when you're providing those grades, MF, don't do it numerically. As Mary Brennan Stich suggests, "It just sounds a lot better to say 'I have a C average' than it is to say that 'I have a 1.9 GPA' or 'My GPA is 2.2.' And if you're near the median in your class, simply say, 'I'm near the middle of the class' and leave it at that." And she also discourages you from dwelling on *why* your grades aren't what they could be. "Whenever you go on about a terrible illness, or a divorce, or an ill family member, or an accident you had, you're keeping the employer focused on your grades, and that's not where you want them to be."

So, where are you? You've breezily conveyed your non-numerical exam performance. What then? Talk immediately about how it is that you can advance the employers' goals. Mary Brennan Stich suggests that you think ahead of time about what it is you *do* bring to the table, other than your grades. "Do you have practical experience in clinical work? Do you have experience that shows you'd be good at helping people solve problems? Or did you work before law school or do you work full-time now, so that you can tell an employer that you bring with you a level of maturity that many law students don't have? Or do you learn the ropes quickly? There is nothing that makes an employer happier than hearing you say that because of things you've done *outside* of your exam work, you can hit the ground running." What does all of this tell you, MF? That it's not what your GPA is, but the way you focus on what you can do for the employer, *regardless* of your grades. The Job Goddess is aware that most law students don't believe that anything matters except grades, but as Mary Brennan Stich explains, "Demeanor and composure are what it's all about."

Some law students cut the tension about grades in interviews by leading with humor when they're asked about their grades. A response of which the Job Goddess is particularly fond is, "I'm the kind of student who makes the top half of the class possible." Another chestnut is, "Boy, am I glad I don't have to show my parents my report card anymore." Lines like this can work for you, MF, but Mary Brennan Stich cautions you against humor if you're not good at it; if you're not a joke teller naturally, talking about your grades isn't the time to wheel in your Don Rickles impression. You'll find that the words will leave your mouth and crash to the ground before they reach the interviewer, and you'll both sit in a sullen, embarrassed silence.

So that's the interview approach. What should you do in a resume or letter? Law schools differ in their advice about when to avoid putting your grades on your resume, but bear in mind that if you don't include them, employers will assume they aren't good. Face it, MF, if you're the employer and you see a resume *sans* grades, your first thought isn't going to be, "Hmm, this student must be on Law Review." The advice on grades in interviews applies here, too; make sure that your resume highlights what you *have* done well in, whether it's a clinic, or part-time work for a professor, or volunteering, or anything else that gives you skills you can state explicitly in your resume. In your cover letter, you similarly want to avoid the grades bandwagon. Mary Brennan Stich suggests that you "Avoid explaining your grades in writing. Instead, be prepared to talk about them in the interview, once you've gotten your foot in the door." In your letter, as in the interview, focus on those skills, skills, skills you bring to the table for the employer. Remember, MF, an employer won't hire you because of the excuses you make about what you *don't* have, but what you *do* have. The Job Goddess promises you that if you do that, MF—in letters, resumes, interviews, even in casual conversations—employers will overlook that GPA more quickly than you'd ever have dared to dream possible.

ETERNALLY YOURS,

The Job Goddess

What Should I Say When They Ask Me How Much Money I Want to Make?

Dear Job Goddess,

Every interviewer has asked the same questions, and I'm stumped. What is the correct response to, "What are your salary expectations?" and "What is your salary history?" The problem is that I'm 37, an evening division student with significant business experience, but I recognize that if I get the legal employment I'm looking for, I won't be starting in the $75,000 range where I am currently. What should I say?

sincerely, JN

P.S. I loved your Guerrilla Tactics book.

Dear JN,

The Job Goddess loves the salary question, because it's quite obvious what the honest answer is: "I want to make a million bucks a year." Who doesn't? Of course, you already know, JN, that you can't say that.

Let's take a look at the rock and the hard place which are behind the salary question. On the one hand, if you say, "Oh, I'll be happy with anything," you worry about undervaluing yourself, you imagine that the employer is secretly laughing at you for your apparent lack of self-esteem, and—worst of all—ultimately fear you might actually receive an offer that would rival the take-home pay from the drive-thru window.

On the other hand, if you name a figure three standard deviations *above* what the employer intends to pay, you run the risk of losing an offer for being unrealistic— or not getting an offer at all, because the employer figures you won't accept the salary that goes with the position.

Fortunately for the Job Goddess, it is very easy for you to get around the salary issue. It requires about five minutes of advance research. What you want to do is to contact the career services office at your law school (or make friends with the career services office at the nearest law school to you right now), and ask for the National Association of Law Placement ("NALP") salary statistics covering the kind of job you're looking for. Fortunately for you, JN, NALP breaks down its statistics into almost block-by-block detail, covering not only what you ought to make as a starting point for any given kind of legal job and size of legal employer anywhere in the country, but also what you can anticipate making in year two, year three, and so on.

Once you are armed with these statistics, what you want to do is to throw a $10,000 range around the average figure, so that when you are asked what your salary expectations are, you can offer the following answer: "My research shows that starting salaries in this city for employers like you is in the $35,000 to $45,000 range, and I'd be happy with that." What does this do? A whole flock of brilliant things for you. First of all, it shows off the fact that you've done some research on the employer, and that is *always* applauded. It also alerts the employer to what others of their size and general makeup offer, and so if this particular employer was thinking of offering less than that, it will make them think twice and perhaps goose up their offer to fall into line with their competitors. And it gives them some wiggle room for a specific figure.

The second part of your question, about your salary history, seems a bit trickier, but in fact you've already taken much of the sting out of it if you give the answer on salaries that the Job Goddess has just provided for you. After all, what is the interviewer thinking if you mention your current $75,000 annual haul? "Holy cow, this guy is *never* going to accept a job making less than that. And if he *does*, he's going to quit the moment he finds a job that pays more!" If your answer suggests that you've researched salaries ahead of time, you have removed much of the worry for the employer. You can cement that even further by adding something along the lines of, "I thought long and hard about taking a pay cut, but frankly, I went to law school because I wanted to be a lawyer, and I wouldn't be wasting your time if I weren't dedicated to doing exactly that." Then immediately follow up your answer with a question about something unrelated to salary, so that you aren't sucked into a long back-and-forth on a topic that doesn't further your goal of selling what you bring to the table for this particular employer. After all, the skills you learned gathering your valuable business experience is what makes you so attractive, not the money you made learning it.

Incidentally, JN—and you didn't ask it, but the Job Goddess realizes that there are many people with your concerns who *would* have asked this—never bring up the salary issue before you have an offer on the table. The Job Goddess has heard of more than one hapless interviewee who punted a sure job offer by asking the seemingly innocent question, "So what's the salary?" Set the hook and get the offer first—and worry about the money afterwards.

ETERNALLY YOURS,

The Job Goddess

P.S.: The Job Goddess loves the fact that you love her book *Guerrilla Tactics for Getting the Legal Job of Your Dreams*, and that you provided her with yet another opportunity to mention it.

What Do I Say When Large Firms Ask Me What Specialty I Want?

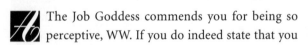

DEAR JOB GODDESS,

I've been interviewing with large firms, and I'm worried about my answer to a question they always ask me, which is "Which specialty do you want to practice?" What if I mention a specialty where they don't have any openings? I feel like if I make a mistake, I won't get an offer. How do I handle it?

WW, Florida

DEAR WW,

The Job Goddess commends you for being so perceptive, WW. If you do indeed state that you want to practice, say, international law, and the employer you're interviewing with only has openings in its labor and litigation departments, well . . . the Job Goddess would be misleading you to suggest that you should anticipate an offer.

Frankly, WW, the very interview question itself is a minefield, at least when you're talking about large firms. Why is that? Well, the most likely source of information about what a firm does—namely, Martindale-Hubbell, and its brethren—doesn't rank specialties in terms of which are growing and therefore likely to require an additional set of eager hands like yours. Furthermore, the Job Goddess has found, in talking with associates by way of researching *America's Greatest Places to Work With a Law Degree,* (ah, she'll do anything to work in a plug), that most large-firm associates wind up in specialties they didn't even realize **existed** before they became permanent associates. So the question of "What do you want to do?" is, simply put, a trap for the unwary.

Such traps are the Job Goddess's delight, as you know. For advice on this issue the Job Goddess turned to Marci Cox, the Career Services Director at the University of Miami School of Law, and prior to that a large-firm lawyer herself. Her advice? "When you go into a large firm interview, as early as you possibly can, ask the interviewer, 'In your opinion, which of the firm's specialties are growing the fastest?' The interviewer will give you a short menu, and armed with this, when you are subsequently asked, 'Which specialty are you interested in practicing?' you can respond, 'Well, of the ones you mentioned, I'd say that I'm most attracted to . . . ' and then name the one that seems most attractive to you. You may want to follow up fairly quickly by asking the interviewer which specialty (s)he practices (if you don't know already, from your research), and ask how (s)he chose it. In most cases the interviewer will say that (s)he didn't have a firm idea of which specialty (s)he'd wind up in. This way, you haven't closed yourself off to an offer by stating a specialty that's got enough players, and you've gotten the spotlight off of yourself as quickly as possible.

Is this a bit of sleight of hand, WW? Yes, it is. And the Job Goddess warns her minions who are reading over your metaphorical shoulder, WW, that a large firm is the only place where this kind of wishy-washiness is appropriate. In the vast majority of legal interviews, an answer that smacks of "Oh, I'll do anything" suggests that you lack self-awareness and you are desperate, neither of which are attractive attributes in a new hire. A large firm is a world unto itself, and should be treated accordingly. And if an offer from a large firm is what you seek, WW, then the Job Goddess's only happiness is to see that you get it.

ETERNALLY YOURS,

The Job Goddess

How Do I Answer When They Ask Me if I'm Willing to Work Eighty Hours a Week?

DEAR JOB GODDESS,

I've been doing some interviewing and a few times the interviewer has asked me if I'm willing to work long hours. One interviewer actually came out and said, "Are you willing to work 80 hours a week?" How should I respond?

TL, New York

Dear TL,

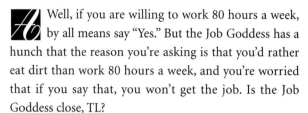 Well, if you are willing to work 80 hours a week, by all means say "Yes." But the Job Goddess has a hunch that the reason you're asking is that you'd rather eat dirt than work 80 hours a week, and you're worried that if you say that, you won't get the job. Is the Job Goddess close, TL?

So what should you do? As Susan Kalb Weinberg, Director of Career Services at the University of Michigan School of Law, suggests, "If you don't want those hours, you really have to say 'No.' But don't end your answer there. Go on to say something along the lines of 'I wouldn't clock 80 hours a week just to do it. Instead, I'm more oriented towards projects than hours. I have always met deadlines. And in a limited situation, like a big trial, I would be willing to put in long hours. But on a routine basis, no. I can't imagine I would be a good lawyer if I worked 80 hours a week every week—I would burn out.'" In other words, don't suggest that you're not willing to kick in and be a member of the team—ooh, there's that word 'team' that employers love so much. Team team team. Mention it in interviews as often as you can, TL. But don't lie and pretend that you're willing to accept a time commitment that you are truly unwilling to tolerate.

Having said that, take what employers suggest as time commitments with a grain of salt. As Susan Kalb Weinberg points out, "Some firms like to come off as though they're the Navy SEALS, and that you've got to be a 'real man' to make it there. It creates a kind of mystique for them. In my experience, the ones who suggest that they're really tough aren't as tough as they seem. And on the other end of the scale, firms who market themselves as humane may really consider themselves less than that." Instead of focusing on hours, TL, Susan Weinberg suggests that you focus on questions like "Did you like the people? Or the work?" And do all the research you can ahead of time about any particular employer. Talk to your career services director and/or alumni relations director at school, and ask if they know what kinds of time commitments are involved with different employers you're considering, or if they know anybody who might know. You can't ask about hours in an interview, because you'll sound like a slacker, but you can be sly and go the career services route ahead of time. And once you have an offer, all bets are off; go ahead and query young associates about the kinds of hours they put in, if it's important to you.

If you have significant time commitments outside of your career, TL, you can easily weave that into your job search scheme. For instance, if you really only want to work 30 to 40 hours a week, those legal jobs do exist—the Job Goddess profiled some of them in her book, *America's Greatest Places to Work With a Law Degree*—but there are usually sacrifices to be made in terms of upward potential. Such jobs can be wonderfully fulfilling, and you may enjoy them very much, but again, it's a tradeoff only you can make, TL. After all, the only kind of job that has guaranteed punch-in-punch-out times is an hourly job. When you think about it, as Susan Weinberg points out, "When you're talking about a salaried job, it's very rare to find one that requires a basic 40-hour week."

And frankly, even though the Job Goddess realizes you might not look at it this way right now, an employer who comes right out in an interview and asks you that might be doing you a favor. After all, if the job requires 80 hours a week and your concept of your dream job requires many fewer hours than that, the interviewer is really telling you, "If we make you an offer, for God's sake don't take it!" You'll be miserable, TL, and the Job Goddess doesn't want you to be miserable. She wants you to be brilliantly happy. If you are honest with yourself about the commitment you're willing to make (both in terms of hours and results), you research employers to see who fits that profile, and you think expansively about the sacrifices you're willing to make for the hours you want to work—you *will* be brilliantly happy!

ETERNALLY YOURS,

The Job Goddess

———

Should I Wear My Wedding Ring to Interviews?

Dear Job Goddess,

 Should I, a married woman in my mid-20s, take off my wedding band when I interview? Employers always notice it, and I firmly believe that it has worked against me in the vast majority of my interviews. However, if I take it off and then get offered the job, I'm afraid my employer would deeply resent me once (s)he found out the truth. I'm afraid that I would be seen as untrustworthy. What should I do?

SO, Illinois

Dear SO,

The Job Goddess's first thought on reading your letter, SO, was to ask herself what your wedding band might look like that it attracts so much attention. The Job Goddess herself had informed her boyfriend that she was willing to get engaged as soon as he was willing to buy her an engagement ring in the shape of a skull, with diamonds for eyes. (By the by, he didn't proffer a skull-shaped ring this fall, but the Goddess said "yes" anyway!)

While the Job Goddess basks in the glow of her engagement, she has nonetheless found the time to devote to pondering your question, which is a very good—and very common—one. And the Job Goddess sadly agrees that it is well possible that certain employers look askance at you once they notice "the ring." But if we step back a moment and think about why that might be so, your strategy for handling this uncomfortable situation becomes a little clearer.

SO, when interviewers notice your ring, coupled with the fact that you are in the bloom of young-womanhood, many of them will think: "Aha! She's married. She's going to have children any day now, and quit her job." At which point said employer envisions wasting its money and time in training you, SO. It's the Job Goddess's belief that the well-intentioned law, which at least in some circumstances prohibits interviewers from asking about your family situation, exacerbates this problem, because interviewers can't ask you directly: "Are you going to quit to have kids?" You are left unable to defend yourself in light of what may be a terribly unfair assumption. The notion that you'll leave the employer in short order to raise a family is the proverbial 600-pound gorilla in the room with the interviewer and you.

What to do? Every career services director the Job Goddess knows agrees with Chicago-Kent's Stephanie Rever Chu. "If you really think your wedding band is getting in the way, bring it up the moment you see an interviewer looking at your ring! Say something like, 'I don't know if my being married is an issue for you, but I want to reassure you that I am dedicated to my career.'" You can go on to say that you understand the time demands of a law career with whatever kind of employer you're seeking, and you wouldn't be interviewing with them—and wasting their time—if you weren't serious about this.

As you say these things, SO, make sure that there is no edge in your voice. Be matter-of-fact, smile, and understand the employer's concern while making your point. The Job Goddess assures you that you will earn massive brownie points for putting yourself in the shoes of the employer, and that any problems you have faced with regard to your marital status will quickly dissolve in the face of your candor.

The Job Goddess suspects that you are much happier with coming clean, in a savvy way, than you would be with the alternative, SO—a variation of the old Band-aid-around-the-ring-finger trick associated with philandering traveling salesmen. As Stephanie Rever Chu points out, "This is a situation where you've got to be honest. After all, if the simple fact that you're married ultimately works against you, is this an employer you'd really want to work for? No!"

So keep wearing that wedding band, SO, and confidently explain that you know what's expected of you and you plan to deliver. The Job Goddess is certain that with this approach, you will soon have the opportunity to do so!

ETERNALLY YOURS,

The Job Goddess

"Can I Wear a Pantsuit to an Interview?"

Dear Job Goddess,

I'm going to be interviewing with law firms on campus at school. Do you think times have changed enough so that it would be all right if I wore a pantsuit to interviews?

PV, Minneapolis

Dear PV,

If you are a man, PV, the Job Goddess believes that wearing pants to interviews is not only acceptable, but mandatory. But of course the Job Goddess realizes that you are, in fact, a woman, which is why you're curious about the pants issue.

The Job Goddess understands the nature of the dilemma, PV. For one thing, in more and more law offices, female attorneys routinely show up in tailored pantsuits. Furthermore, if you've attended any employer panels at school, you may well have heard individual attorneys saying that they would have no problem with women showing up in pants for interviews. Marci Cox, the Career Services Director at the University of Miami School of Law, recalls that as a litigator she once showed up in court wearing a fire-engine red pantsuit. The judge not only didn't mind but, in fact, complimented her on her outfit.

So where does this leave you in interviews? Exactly where you were to start with: that is, playing the odds.

While it is unquestionably true that there are interviewers who would not mind—and in fact would welcome—a break from seeing a sea of law students in conservative attire, it's impossible to determine who those interviewers *are* ahead of time. And that's why it pays to dress at least relatively conservatively.

There are at least three issues to keep in mind with interview garb, however. If you are in the rare and fortunate situation of knowing how a particular interviewer feels about interview attire—for instance, you've seen the interviewer speak and they've expressly stated that they are bored by conservative suits in interviews, or your career services director personally knows the interviewer's preferences, or you know someone who knows the interviewer and can give you the inside skinny on such matters—then by all means wear something that, while still professional, shows more of your fashion flare.

It's also true that different kinds of attire are appropriate in different parts of the country. While these are broad generalizations, reports from the Job Goddess's correspondents with law schools and employers nationwide suggest that, for instance, the Pacific Northwest is more casual, Southern employers prefer to see more makeup on women than do employers in other parts of the country, and New York employers expect you to be more fashion-forward.

Another issue to consider is the kind of employer with whom you are interviewing, PV. You say "law offices," but the Job Goddess realizes this covers a broad swath of potential employers. For a Wall Street firm, a very expensive, tailored suit would be appropriate. For a public interest employer, on the other hand, you'd create entirely the wrong impression by showing up in an Armani.

The bottom line on bottoms, PV? Unless you absolutely, positively know differently with a particular interviewer, save your pantsuits for the time when you've already nailed down the job, and identified that the people who wear pants at the office are at least some-times female.

ETERNALLY YOURS,

The Job Goddess

The Party's Over

Post-Interview Issues

"Is It Totally Unacceptable to Go on Looking For Something Better if I've Already Accepted a Job Offer I'm Not Exactly Excited About?"

Dear Job Goddess,

I have a question involving ethics. I have in my mind that I would like to practice law in another part of the country. However, anxiety over getting a job led me to accept an offer in the city where I go to law school. I have a year before I am to begin work. Would it be totally unacceptable to continue looking for a job in the interim, and, if something else comes up, tell the firm that I've changed my mind?

HB, Maryland

Dear HB,

The Job Goddess suspects that you already know the answer to your "is-it-unacceptable" question. She will briefly discuss it with you nonetheless. But then she will address what's really sticking in your emotional craw, HB, which is this—How do I weasel out of a job that I don't really want, and find one that I *do* want?

Before we get to that much thornier question, the Job Goddess will dispense with the answer you already know. Yes, it *would* be unacceptable to slink around behind your future employer's back, even as they shine up your office nameplate and prepare your professional layette, seeking out the career equivalent of Bo Derek in

156

the movie "10." The moral reason is best illustrated by putting the shoe on the other foot, as explained by Ann Skalaski of the University of Florida School of Law. "Think about how *you'd* feel if a firm that made you an offer subsequently called you back and said, 'We've found somebody we like better than you. We want to revoke your offer and hire them.'" You'd be horrified, and rightly so. The same goes for your employer.

If that ethical consideration isn't enough to convince you, HB, a practical one might. As soon as you renege on your offer, your reputation is shot. The legal community you thought was so huge will shrink to nothing, and the employer you left at the altar will know somebody who knows somebody in the city where you want to go. On top of *that*, your classmates will certainly know what you did, and as Ann Skalaski points out, "Your professional reputation starts at school. You never know whether that guy you had a beer with will turn out to be a judge. You can't afford a bad reputation!"

Now that the Job Goddess has lifted that ethical burden from her heavenly chest, she will give you the advice she knows you secretly want. You have two options, HB, and you will have to judge the circumstances yourself to determine which is more appropriate.

The first is to sit down with your intended employer, *now*, and come clean. While you will have to come up with the precise wording yourself, tracking the truth as you explained it to the Job Goddess wouldn't hurt. Tell them face-to-face that in your heart of hearts you really want to live in Laredo (or wherever), and that your conscience stops you from working for them with less than complete enthusiasm. Tell them that you accepted the offer in good faith, but now you have doubts you can't resolve. This is no time to be defensive, HB. 'Prostrate with regret' is closer to the posture you want to assume. Thank them for their confidence in you and tell them that under any other circumstances you'd love to work for them, but you can't.

Their reaction may take several forms. They may be really angry. Let them vent. Tell them in their shoes you'd be angry, too, but you wanted them to know the truth as soon as you yourself realized it, with as much time as possible to find a replacement for you. They may act hurt—they **will** be hurt. Again, leave them to it. Acknowledge that you aren't proud of yourself, but you want to be as up front with them as they are with you. And tell them that maybe you're making a huge mistake, maybe working in Seattle (or wherever) won't be what you expect, but you wouldn't want to start your career with less than full enthusiasm.

What does this do for you, HB? No matter how upset or angry they may be in the moment, they'll respect you for your honesty, and the courage it took to say what you said, and in person, no less. They may question your judgment but they won't question your integrity. After all, law students rarely come clean in situations like yours, HB—You'll be a breath of fresh air.

Of course, the downside to this approach is that you're giving up a sure thing in favor of a dream, HB. But if your misgivings are strong enough—and you read and follow the advice in the Job Goddess's wonderful best-seller, *Guerrilla Tactics for Getting the Legal Job of Your Dreams*—you may find that it is a risk worth taking.

Option B would be to bite the bullet, stay put for a year or two, and then lateral into your dream job in the Emerald City (or wherever). While that's not totally being honest with your currently intended employer, there are three things to be said for it. One is that you may find that you really love the job after all, which the Job Goddess supposes would be the best, if not the most likely, of all possible worlds. You can always vacation in San Antonio (or wherever), and that may sate your travelin' jones.

Even if you *do* have it in mind that you'll be leaving in a year or two, you wouldn't be the first law student to view their first job as an apprenticeship. Heck, based on the Job Goddess's research for her fabulous book,

America's Greatest Places to Work With a Law Degree, you wouldn't be the first-millionth law student to do that. And finally, you could use that year or two to gain valuable experience and expertise for your **next** job. You told the Job Goddess about your anxiety over being able to find a job in Phoenix (or wherever). As you may already know, the lateral market for lawyers is booming, and a job that seems unattainable now will be far easier to get with a bit of experience under your professional belt.

So there you have it, HB. Come clean and roll the dice now, or hunker down for a couple of years that will be over before you know it. But whatever you do, don't sneak around behind your betrothed employer's back. Whatever damage it would do to your professional reputation (and it **would**) concerns the Job Goddess less than how it would impact your opinion of yourself, HB, and that's something you can't afford to sacrifice.

ETERNALLY YOURS,

The Job Goddess

———

If a Law Firm Promises to Call Me Back and Never Does . . . Should I Make the Call?

Dear Job Goddess,

A few months ago, I interviewed with a law firm. It went really well, and the attorney I interviewed with told me that she would really try to get me on board with the firm, hoping she could convince the powers that be that I should be hired. Shortly thereafter, the firm held a partners' meeting where I was on the agenda. I haven't heard anything since that time. Even though it's been a few months, I haven't gotten an offer from anybody else. Should I call the firm again and express my interest? After all, it's been months and I haven't heard from them. And I confess, I've been too chicken to call; I did try once, but nobody ever called me back. Should I try again?

SE, Illinois

Dear SE,

In a word—yes. The Job Goddess realizes this seems, offhand, like telling you to put on a hamburger bathing suit and jump into a shark tank, but it isn't that way at all. To understand why, SE, you've got to appreciate all of the perfectly understandable, not-rejecting-you reasons why you might not have received a call. As Susan Richey, Career Services Director at Franklin Pierce Law Center (and an attorney before that), points out, "Not receiving a call doesn't mean anything! It certainly doesn't mean they hated you. For instance, they may be waiting for the business they need to support your salary. When I was starting out, a law firm once told me, 'We're counting on a huge piece of litigation, and if we get it, we'll need you.' There are many firms in that position, but often they won't **tell** you what's going on."

On the other hand, of course, you don't want to be a pest. Susan Richey says that in order to walk the fine line between showing enthusiasm and being a bother, "If they haven't given you a date when they'll contact you, wait until two weeks after your interview, and then call and say, 'I really enjoyed myself there, and wanted to check on the status of my application.' Most good recruiting coordinators will give you a date when you can call back, but if they don't, ask if you'll be a bother if you call back."

If the law firm you're interviewing with is too small for a recruiting coordinator, it could well be that the lawyers there have simply been too busy to give your situation the attention it deserves. When you call the firm and speak to the hiring partner's secretary, you could well be speaking to somebody who is up to her rhymes-with-"mass" in alligators. If she doesn't give you an answer, or says something like "I don't know where your application is," Susan Richey advises you to ask if it would be a problem if you called back in a week's time. If a week's not okay, the secretary is likely to give you a date that *is*.

As your situation illustrates, SE, it's important to keep the ball in your court whenever possible. That is, keep the calling privilege for yourself. As Sue Richey advises, "Instead of just leaving a voice mail message for them to call you back, say that you'll try back in a week, and leave them your number in case they want to call you in the meantime."

If time drags on and there is still no decision, think about contacting the person with whom you got along the best to see what else—if anything—you can do to further your cause. Again, couch your request in terms of how much you liked the firm and how you'd like to make a contribution; now is not the time to say, "Honestly, I wouldn't care so much except that I haven't found anything else and I'm getting desperate."

What is the downside risk of this entire approach, SE? There isn't one. As Susan Richey points out, "If they're going to reject you, they won't reject you any harder because you followed up." As the Job Goddess stressed at the outset, there are many reasons why you might not receive an offer that have nothing to do with whether they liked you or not. And even if their reasons *did* involve you, remember that it's only their *impression* of you, how you did in a single interview, and whatever you showed them of your credentials in the form of resumes, cover letters, writing samples, and the like. They didn't reject you, the flesh-and-blood person, SE—and no employer ever has that power unless you give it to them. The Job Goddess trusts that you won't.

ETERNALLY YOURS,

The Job Goddess

No Thank You to 'Thank You Notes'?

DEAR JOB GODDESS,

Should I send thank you notes after interviews? I always thought you were supposed to, but now some people say you don't have to. I hope that is true because I find it very difficult to know what to say.

JO, Alabama

DEAR JO,

The Job Goddess knows that you will be delighted to find out that—for once—something difficult is not worthwhile, after all!

Emily Post may be appalled, but current opinion on "thank you" notes is this: in most cases, don't bother.

Why is that? As Mary Brennan Stich, Assistant Dean for Career Services at St. Mary's University School of

162

Law, and formerly a partner on the recruiting committee at a large law firm, explains: "Thank you letters make absolutely no difference to anybody I know. The recruiting committee at our firm never even looked at them. Run-of-the-mill, cookie-cutter thank you notes, written just for the sake of writing them, are a complete waste of time." In fact, JO, the Job Goddess has heard more than once that thank you notes often hurt more than they help. "Misspelling someone's name, exhibiting a poor writing style, things like that can actively work against you," says Mary Brennan Stich.

So by and large, JO, you needn't bother with a thank you. That covers on-campus interviews and most callbacks, but there are, of course, exceptions. If you got along particularly well with an interviewer, you *really* hit it off, jot that person a note, handwritten, stating your delight and citing whatever it was that made the interview so memorable, in order to make the note a personal one. And if the interviewer asked you to follow up with something, for instance, an article you've written or a clipping you mentioned in the interview, of course you should do so—but then, that's not a thank you note in the strictest sense, is it?

If you feel compelled to send follow-up correspondence by way of keeping you fresh in the mind of an employer or any other useful contact, that's entirely possible to do without ever sending out a thank you note. Here's how. Make notes after each of your interviews, jotting down any particular interest that the interviewer mentioned, or anything else about them that is obvious from their office decor, like a fly-fishing trophy, or a bit of framed Civil War memorabilia. Let's say, for instance, that you interview with Cleopatra Nile and notice an interesting stuffed snake—an asp—on her desk. When you notice it and say "Nice asp," Cleopatra mentions that she has a live asp at home that she keeps as a pet. After the interview, of course you'd note that interest. Subsequently, you're surfing the web or perusing newspapers or magazines, and you come across an item involving that interest, for instance, a new low-fat asp food that just came out. Download or clip it, and send it to Cleopatra with a note saying hello, mentioning that she might enjoy the item, and updating her briefly on what you're up to. This is a terrific, and non-pesty, way to keep your name at the front of anyone's mind. In fact, law students have been known to endear themselves to the Job Goddess by finding out that she loves to cook, and surfing the web for interesting recipes for her.

Mary Brennan Stich also recommends that when you see an item in the newspaper mentioning an employer with whom you've interviewed, you should clip that mention and send it to the person you know at the firm. People always enjoy reading about themselves, and often they won't have seen the item until you send it to them.

As you've noticed, JO, the Job Goddess has strayed somewhat from thank you notes and well into the territory of ongoing correspondence. She does this merely by way of reassuring you that the odious task of drafting thank you notes is largely one that you can—happily—avoid.

E T E R N A L L Y   Y O U R S ,

The Job Goddess

All Dressed Up and Nowhere to Go

Getting a Job When You Graduate Without One

Looking for Law While You're Working Full-Time at Wal-Mart

Dear Job Goddess,

I graduated from law school and recently passed the bar, and I am working now in the marketing department of a corporation. My job gives me some time to do legal research, but I worry I'm not getting the experience I need. I really want to find work as an attorney, but there are some obstacles for me. I went to school in another state so alumni are scarce where I'm living. Also, I can't afford to quit my job and volunteer because I need my salary to pay my bills. How can I earn a living and still make the contacts I need?

SS, California

Dear SS,

No nearby alumni? Can't afford to volunteer? Pshaw, SS—"pshaw" being the suitable retort here, even though the Job Goddess admits she doesn't know exactly how you'd actually pronounce the word. No matter. The Job Goddess will tell you exactly what you need to do to find work you do want, even if you can't drop everything and hitchhike the thousand miles to find your nearest fellow alum. In fact, the Job Goddess will even set fire to the circus hoops you want her to jump through, by assuming that you can't let your current employer know you're looking for another job.

166

You don't say what kind of law you want to practice, but it doesn't matter. For the sake of argument, let's say it's dog bite law. Contact the local bar association, and find out who runs the dog bite specialty section, and when the section meets. Go to the next meeting, and introduce yourself to the section chairperson. Volunteer to help out, whether it's researching an issue or making a presentation to the section on some cutting-edge topic, or anything else. The Job Goddess knows a recent law school graduate who got the criminal defense job he wanted by researching the status of polygraphs in his state, and making a presentation about it to the criminal defense section of his local bar. If you don't feel comfortable making presentations, SS, any other kind of volunteering—for instance, helping to set up meetings or find speakers—will give you an excuse to talk to people who do exactly what you want to do, and turn strangers into contacts.

You should also expand your reading list. Find out what practitioners in your specialty read, and start reading those publications yourself. If you read an article that interests you, write to the lawyer who wrote it, compliment them on the article, and ask for advice on breaking into their field. As a writer herself, the Job Goddess can assure you that peppering writers with compliments makes them very open to helping you. In the same vein, let's say you stumble across an article in some legal periodical about someone who does what you want to do. Contact them and tell them you read about them, and would love advice about following in their footsteps. Will ***everybody*** fall at your feet if you do as the Job Goddess suggests? Perhaps not. But enough of them ***will*** that you will make all of the contacts you need, SS. And remember, every time you make a contact this way, even if that particular contact can't help you, you need to do two things: ask if they know anyone else who might help you, and thank them profusely for any advice, information, or referrals they ***do*** offer.

Getting the idea, SS? You can see the theme here. You find things that you feel comfortable doing, that also, coincidentally, get you in touch with people who can help you. The Job Goddess is confident that by acting on any one of these ideas, or ones you generate yourself, you'll be pleasantly surprised by how quickly you can get out of that marketing department and into the legal job of your dreams.

ETERNALLY YOURS,

The Job Goddess

Out of Law School, Out of Work: How to Face the Inevitable, "What Have You Been Doing...?"

DEAR JOB GODDESS,

I graduated from law school a semester early, figuring that I'd have a leg up in the job market. Yeah, right! I've been out of work ever since graduation, and that's been more than six months. It's getting to the point where I dread talking to anybody about a job because I don't know how to deal with the question I know I'm going to get: "What have you been doing since graduation?" Job Goddess, help! What should I do?

Desperate in Detroit

Dear Desperate,

Not what you're doing *now,* that's for sure . . . if the Job Goddess's hunch is correct, and you're trying to forget your troubles with a combination of daytime talk shows, cheese puffs, and beer.

In fact, you've already done at least one very smart thing, in summoning the Job Goddess. She is very sympathetic to your plight because although it is not widely known, in the days when she was a mere mortal, the Job Goddess herself was—ahem—"at liberty" for some time after law school. So she knows what you're thinking. No matter what the interviewer is saying, in your mind they're **really** thinking "Loser! Loser! Loser!" And why is that, Desperate? Because lurking in a horrible dungeon in your mind is a nagging little gremlin, telling you, "Maybe you really *are* a loser."

The Job Goddess assures you that you are *not* a loser, Desperate. For a start, you're not alone. More than half of law students graduate from law school without a job, although virtually everybody is employed within a year after graduation. So you may consider what you are enduring as a typical, albeit unpleasant, rite of passage.

But, you plead, what should you *do?* "You have to do whatever it takes to keep your hand in the legal pie," according to Laura Rowe Lane, Associate Director of Career Development at George Washington University Law School. Get involved in things that will help you forget about your plight *and* rub elbows with people who can help you. For instance, contact your alma mater's career services office and see if your school participates in Pro Bono Students America ("PBSA"), an organization that matches up students and graduates with volunteer legal work. The Job Goddess has had many favorable reports about PBSA projects, hearing them frequently characterized as "a blast"—they'll help you make contacts, give you valuable experience, and convince you that you really *can* do great work.

If PBSA isn't available to you, improvise! Contact the local bar association, and ask to volunteer for committees that interest you. Or ask if the local bar association has a referral service for volunteer work. Again—an excellent way to meet people who can help you, and get your feet wet as well. Also contact local law schools to find out about CLE classes being taught locally. This is a great way to show your interest in a specialty, bone up on what's new in the law, and again, to meet potential employers. Or consider doing some legal temping, for all of the same reasons. You wouldn't be the first person to turn a temporary job into a permanent offer.

In short, you may be feeling career-challenged right now, Desperate, but if you do as the Job Goddess says, you'll feel better about yourself, *and* you'll find a wonderful job, to boot. The Job Goddess asks for no more than the satisfaction of helping you accomplish exactly that.

ETERNALLY YOURS,

The Job Goddess

How Do I Get a Job After Failing the Bar . . . Three Times?

DEAR JOB GODDESS,

 I have not passed the bar in three attempts. Every time I miss the mark by about 10 points. However, this 'failure' has put a damper on my getting a job. Some firms won't hire me because I haven't passed the bar, and others won't because even though they don't need me to pass the bar, they're afraid that I'm going to take it again, pass, and leave. I am smart and a hard worker. I have always been an overachiever and never failed at anything, and now I am feeling the crunch of not getting a job. I have postponed my loans (temporarily) and my mother is being very gracious with money. However, the money is likely to run thinner if I don't get a job soon. Any suggestions?

AM, Florida

Dear AM,

It would seem at the outset that a question like yours would push the Job Goddess's eternal optimism envelope. But while hard questions may be the quicksands of the law, the Job Goddess only attained goddess status by shrinking the most Olympian obstacles down to size. And your difficulty, AM, is one that you can overcome in three steps.

First of all, you have to strip away the emotional issues and look at what not passing the bar actually means to any employer you might talk to. As the UCLA Law School's Career Services Director Amy Berenson points out, "What do employers really care about when it comes to the bar? There are really only two issues. For one thing, if you're not licensed, you can't represent people in court, or sign pleadings, or represent yourself as a licensed attorney. That's it. But the second thing is that employers will question whether you're competent. To overcome that, you've got to point to things that show that you *are* competent."

How exactly do you do that, AM? First of all, you must develop a script to handle the question you know is going to arise. Namely, what the heck is going on with you and the bar exam? By way of spadework, you have to make a list of all of your accomplishments, and every person in a supervisory position who would have good things to say about you—be it professors for whom you've done research, or any legal clinic professors, or any practitioners with whom you have experience. As Amy Berenson advises you, "Don't hang your head and say you've failed the bar three times. Instead, say something along these lines: 'It's a strange fluke. I've done XYZ in school, I've had positive recommendations from previous employers. I'm just baffled by this. I know I will pass. In the meantime, what shows my research skills are A and B and C. And I encourage you to speak with my previous employers, because they will tell you I can write a great brief and/or do great research and/or I am well-spoken when it comes to interviewing clients and witnesses, and/or any other skills you have that are relevant.'" Come up with your own words, AM, and practice your script until you can say it without apologizing, and with your head held high, a confident tone of voice, and looking directly at the interviewer. You see, AM, this is not a matter of a reality you can't escape. This is a matter of salesmanship, pointing out why it is that even with this hiccup in your otherwise sterling record, you are a real asset to employers.

With your script memorized, what kind of work should you look for? As you point out, employers who don't require bar passage haven't hired you for fear that when you *do* pass, you'll quit. To overcome that problem, don't look for permanent positions! In fact, as Amy Berenson recommends, "The most important thing for you to do while you try to pass the bar is to keep your skills up. For that, your best bet is probably a combination of temping a few days a week, and then volunteering a couple of days a week. To find the temp work, you've got several options. You can contact an agency that places legal temps. With these kinds of agencies you'll typically do document production and so forth. Another option is to go to your career services office and look for listings for firms seeking people for research projects. And while they're typically looking for second-year clerks, you can do anything a second year can do, and on top of that, firms that have these kinds of projects typically need somebody in a hurry, and you're in a perfect position to respond immediately. Another option is to take on research projects with sole practitioners. To find them, you can either look in the Yellow Pages and write a letter offering your services, or call or visit if you're sufficiently bold. Or talk to your career services director, and find leads to sole practitioners that way." Are these going to be high-paying jobs, AM? Well, no. But remember, your goal here is to maintain your skills, and in order to do that, Amy Berenson suggests that you "Have to get over the pride issue of low pay." Simply put, what you surrender in cash-in-hand you make up for in crucial career enhancement.

On top of working for pay two or three days a week, Amy Berenson recommends that you volunteer. For instance, check with your local bar association; many of them have pro bono projects and public interest jobs, like interviewing clients, manning a legal hotline, and the like. As Amy Berenson points out, "It's important for you to get experience on your resume, whether full-time or part-time, paid or volunteer."

What will this 'skills-retention' program accomplish? For one thing, AM, it will help you rehabilitate what is likely a very bruised professional ego. By putting your abilities to work, you are proving to yourself and to the professional community that you *can* do everything that's expected of you—regardless of what your obviously meaningless bar results say. And on top of that, you're forming relationships with employers. It may well be that when you do pass the bar—and the Job Goddess is confident that you will—those very employers may need a new associate or know someone who does. Since they'll already know you and what you can do, you'll be at the top of their list. In fact, the temporary work and volunteering you do may open your eyes to a whole variety of law-related positions that may appeal to you even more than practicing law, such that you never even bother to take the bar exam again. Regardless of which path you choose, the Job Goddess promises you that it is your intelligence and work ethic that will guarantee your success in the long run, regardless of the minor setback posed by that pesky bar exam.

ETERNALLY YOURS,

The Job Goddess

Appendix

Excerpt from *America's Greatest Places to Work with a Law Degree*

So when's the last time you got something for nothing? Since I keep telling you about how great my other new book is, I should let you judge for yourself. What follows is the entry for Procter & Gamble, which is in Chapter 8 of *America's Greatest Places to Work With a Law Degree*.

In case you're curious, *America's Greatest Places* includes profiles for a slew of different kinds of employers—law firms, government positions, public interest jobs, corporate jobs, court-related positions—and much more!

In addition to profiles, I also tell you the 19 traits that define a wonderful place to work, how to find (and get) great jobs at small firms, how to handle law school debt, and 130 "Do's" and "Don'ts" that distinguish new lawyers headed for the top.

Turn the page and see what you think . . .

TABLE OF CONTENTS

Procter & Gamble

1 Procter & Gamble Plaza · Cincinnati, OH 45202
Web site: www.pg.com

PROCTER & GAMBLE IN A NUTSHELL . . .

Procter & Gamble ("P&G") is the worldwide leader in marketing consumer products, with sales of approximately $36 billion last year. It ranks 17ᵀᴴ on the *Fortune 500* list of major U.S. industrial and service corporations, and 9ᵀᴴ on *Fortune's* list of most admired companies. And the company was voted one of the top 10 ideal companies to work for in a recent survey of European business graduates.

P&G products can be found in more homes around the world than those of any other company. The Company manufactures and sells more than 300 brands to nearly five billion consumers in over 140 countries. These brands include Tide, Ariel, Crest, Pantene Pro-V, Always, Whisper, Pringles, Pampers, Oil of Olay, and Vicks. Based in Cincinnati, Ohio, P&G has on-the-ground operations in over 70 countries and employs 106,000 people worldwide.

P&G has won all kinds of recognition as a great place to work, including appearances in *Fortune Magazine's* "100 Best Companies To Work For In America" and "World's Most Admired Companies" List. *Fortune* cites, among other things, P&G's groundbreaking profit-sharing plan, which is also one of the most generous in the country: the company contributes up to 25% of pay to employees' retirement fund.

William Procter and James Gamble founded the company in 1837 in Cincinnati, Ohio as a soap and candle company. Incidentally, both of them came to the business under tragic circumstances. William Procter owned a woolen goods shop in London. The shop was a success, but one night it was robbed of its entire inventory. Dispirited, Procter and his wife hied off to America for a new start. Sadly, Mrs. Procter died of cholera as they neared Cincinnati. Procter, heartbroken, stayed in Cincinnati, and opened a candle shop.

James Gamble came to America in 1819, the 16-year-old son of an Irish minister. They intended to settle in Chicago, but on a boat trip down the Ohio River, James became violently ill and the family went to shore in Cincinnati. The Gambles decided to stay in "Porkopolis"—as Cincinnati was known then—and started a successful business making beer, building ships, and trafficking in hogs. James worked for the family business.

Fate brought Procter and Gamble together, in that they married two sisters, Elizabeth Ann and Olivia Norris, in 1934. As new brothers-in-law, they opened a business buying animal fats. They were immensely respected businessmen, and by the Civil War, they had the largest business in town. Ironically the War proved their ticket to an immense national business. They shrewdly foresaw the war and bought tons of rosin at a dollar a barrel, realizing that when war broke out the price would multiply. And it did—it rose to $15 a barrel, and Procter & Gamble was on its way to lasting national prominence. Its business eventually branched into other areas—food products (1911), laundry products (1933), hair care products (1934), health care products (1943), paper products (1957), pharmaceuticals (1978), skin care products (1985), and cosmetics and fragrances (1989).

P&G has been responsible for many innovative technologies and product categories, including the first synthetic laundry detergent (Dreft, 1933), toothpaste with fluoride (Crest, 1955), the first disposable diaper (Pampers, 1961), the first 2-in-1 shampoo/conditioner (Pert Plus, 1986), and the first fat-free, calorie-free cooking oil that provides full taste (Olean, 1996). P&G's goals include doubling unit volume in 10 years, achieving share growth in the majority of its categories, and delivering total shareholder return that ranks P&G over time among the top third of its peer group. Most importantly, P&G's goal is to continue to provide products of superior quality and value to the world's consumers.

P&G has also grown strategically through acquisitions. Significant transactions include Norwich Eaton Pharmaceuticals (1982), Richardson-Vicks (1985), Noxell (1989), Max Factor (1991), and Tambrands (1997).

Incidentally, P&G's biggest early success—Ivory Soap, "the soap that floats"—was the product of an accident. In 1879, Ivory soap was a standard soap that wouldn't float. However, a worker left a stirring machine on too long, working air bubbles into the soap. The air bubbles made the soap float, and instead of throwing it out P&G turned the mistake into an asset. When it took off, all of the other P&G soap formulas were changed as well.

WORD ON THE STREET . . .

"They hire out-of-school for their patent and corporate office."

"I've never heard a bad thing about them. They leave at 5:30 p.m. They get assigned whole divisions. Unless it's very technical, they handle all of the legal work in-house. It's like having your own client. They make good money and get great benefits. They hire nationwide. People just glow about the work and the people there."

"They are great for families."

NUTS AND BOLTS

Chairman and CEO:

John E. Pepper

General Counsel:

James J. Johnson (J.D., Ohio State Law School)

U.S. Hiring Counsel:

Karl S. Steinmanis, phone: 513-983-4349, e-mail: steinmanis.ks@pg.com

For Patent Counsel:

Koos Rasser, phone: 513-634-6332, e-mail: rasser.jc@pg.com

In-House Counsel's Office . . .

North America: 92 lawyers (In the Cincinnati headquarters, as well as Baltimore, Maryland); Latin America: 26 lawyers; Asia/Pacific: 17 lawyers; Europe: 54 lawyers.

FOREIGN OFFICES WHERE GRADUATES OF AMERICAN LAW SCHOOLS ARE EMPLOYED . . .

P&G's legal organization is globally focused, to mirror the company's focus. It has legal offices in over 50 countries. At any given time, these offices may have lawyers that are citizens of that country, or lawyers that are citizens of another country, or both. The following list shows where U.S. lawyers are located today:

Kobe, Japan (Headquarters of P&G Asia—provides legal and patent counsel for Far East business);

Brussels, Belgium (Headquarters of P&G Europe—provides patent counsel for European business);

Egham, England (Headquarters of P&G UK—provides patent counsel for UK business);

Schwalbach (Headquarters of P&G Germany—provides patent counsel for German business);

Hong Kong, China (Headquarters of P&G China—provides legal counsel for China business);

Buenos Aires, Argentina (Headquarters of P&G Argentina—provides legal counsel for Argentina business);

Mexico City, Mexico (Headquarters of P&G Mexico—provides legal counsel for Mexico business).

HOW TO GET IN TO THE IN-HOUSE COUNSEL'S OFFICE . . .

You can get in as a lateral, a new law school graduate, or as a summer intern. For specific questions, contact Ms. Delores McHargue, Recruiting Secretary, collect, at 513-983-8691.

Laterals: P&G will consider candidates who are up to two years out of law school.

New graduates: P&G hires 13 to 14 law school graduates per year on a world-wide basis into its in-house counsel department. The practice includes the wide spectrum of business law needed to support the company, including corporate, securities, advertising, patents, labor and employment, food and drug, environmental, trademark, and commercial law.

P&G interviews on campus at the following law schools: Duke, Virginia, Vanderbilt, Michigan, Howard, Syracuse, Indiana, Kentucky, Cincinnati and Ohio State. The Company also recruits at job fairs, including the LL.M. Job Fair in New York City, the Loyola Patent Interview Program in Chicago, the Southeastern Law School Consortium Minority Job Fair in Atlanta, and the Hispanic Bar National Consortium Job Fair. In addition, P&G hires from law schools where it doesn't interview on campus—send them a letter and a resume!

What they look for: Excellent academics (top 20% of law school class, Law Review or similar experience, excellent undergraduate academics), significant leadership capabilities, and strengths in initiative and problem-solving skills. In addition, for Patent Counsel the Company looks for people with an undergrad degree in science or engineering and a demonstrated interest in patent law.

P&G is known for providing an employee-friendly environment, and consistent with that, it has very favorable provisions for work-family situations that allow for reduced work schedules.

The starting salary for law school graduates is $$$$ (Over $65,000).

SUMMER INTERNS . . .

P&G hires law students after their second year in law school. Summer associates get a broad legal view of the businesses the in-house counsel's office supports. These areas include advertising, trademarks, patents, employment, environmental, general corporate, litigation, and food and drug work. About 50% of the summer associate's time is focused on research and writing, and the other half is "windshield time"—that is, time spent out of the office attending trials, depositions, client meetings, and the like.

While the summer associates are based in Cincinnati, there are sometimes opportunities for international travel, depending on the work assignments summer associates receive. All summer associates travel domestically as their work requires.

As with permanent hires, P&G looks for top 20% grades, leadership capabilities, and related skills.

The summer associates are paid approximately $1,250 a week.

WHAT DO P&G LAWYERS DO?

Simply put—just about everything!

For one thing, P&G lawyers are involved directly in corporate acquisitions and other major negotiations. In the last several years acquisitions and divestitures totaled more than $3 billion. The Legal Department takes a leadership role on the due diligence and negotiating team, including developing strategy and structuring the transaction. Lawyers draft all documents, negotiate the terms, set up new corporate entities if appropriate, and make necessary federal and state filings.

The Legal Department is involved in contract negotiation and writing for many parts of the Company's business. It handles its own "corporate" practice, including filing of SEC reports, developing the Company's annual Proxy Statement, providing legal advice on officer and director responsibilities and liabilities, structuring internal corporate procedures, and participating directly in corporate financing efforts.

The Legal Department has a major international law practice, involving both participation in foreign investment efforts of P&G and, through Regional General Counsel, the supervision of the legal affairs of the Company's foreign subsidiaries. Some of this work is done in Cincinnati, although there are an additional 90 lawyers employed throughout the world at foreign subsidiaries.

There's also a significant labor/employment law practice. This includes all facets of employment law, including EEO (equal employment opportunities), OSHA, wrongful discharge, and a challenging Labor/NLRB practice—which includes representing the Company in arbitration and Labor Board proceedings. The Legal Department even has an entertainment law practice, since the Company is a large producer of television shows and commercials in the United States.

In the administrative law area, the Legal Department deals with all major federal agencies, doing everything from negotiating and litigating with the agencies to analyzing and commenting on proposed rules.

The Legal Department supervises all litigation involving the Company and its subsidiaries. This includes managing key strategic decisions and participating in trial as well as directly managing discovery and settlement negotiations. Further, there is unlimited opportunity for the legal advocacy many lawyers seek. This comes frequently in administrative hearings, negotiations with outside parties, and negotiations with the government.

P&G expects its attorneys to participate actively in preventing and solving business/legal problems. As attorneys become knowledgeable about P&G's business operations, they are expected to guide proposals so that business objectives can be met within appropriate legal limits. Attorneys frequently take a leadership role in managing business problems that have significant legal considerations.

WHAT LAWYERS SAY ABOUT WORKING FOR P&G . . .

"I have been impressed with the ownership and responsibility given to each new attorney. During my first month here, I immediately started handling direct disputes with our competitors, as well as making significant decisions on advertising, hundred million-dollar contracts, and internal corporate issues. My experience is not unusual. For example, one of my first tasks was to assist in the divestiture of some of our subsidiary corporate holdings in Europe. I was also given direct and sole responsibility over a rather contentious lawsuit with one of our competitors. The instructions I received for that lawsuit were: 'You handle this. If you need help, don't be afraid to ask. Otherwise, let us know how it turns out.' This is incredibly frightening to a new attorney, but exhilarating as well! My responsibilities continue to grow, but every one of my colleagues works with an open door, so I always have help if I need it."

"The thing that I enjoy most about working in the P&G Legal Division is the constant, direct interaction with clients. On a daily basis, I work closely with business people in developing product claims and advertising strategies and structuring acquisitions and divestitures. This broad participation not only enables me to learn more about my client's products, but it also makes me feel like part of the team in growing the overall business."

"The business people here are mostly MBAs from top-ranked programs, and dealing with them on a daily basis is very stimulating."

"The P&G Legal Division is a place where good judgment is one of the most important attributes, and lawyers here are encouraged to use their judgment and knowledge of the business, as well as their legal training, to arrive at creative solutions and issues. For example, one of my current projects involves the development of a product that will be marketed in about two years. I attend all of the product development meetings and counsel the technical and brand management people on what type of support is necessary to support such claims. In this process, as with most of the work I do here, the line between legal and business issues is very blurry. The exciting thing is that people don't care, and welcome and encourage business-related comments from me as well as specific legal advice."

"When I compare notes with my friends from law school, it only reinforces my belief that I made the right decision when I came to P&G's Legal Division. P&G has a reputation for making its people a priority and I have consistently received support and encouragement from my management. I have been given very exciting and diverse assignments since the beginning and my managers have always been careful to make sure that I get the credit for my work when the results come in. I have had the opportunity to directly build relationships with my clients, including executives and senior managers, and I can routinely work with them without having to 'clear everything with my boss' beforehand."

"Several years ago, while I was at work, I found out from my family that my father was seriously ill. I needed to leave right away and travel several hours so that I could see him. When I received the phone call, my mother was concerned that my father did not have a living will, so I offered to draft one right before I left. Several members of the support staff offered to divide up the typing, so that I could leave sooner. I will never forget their kindness."

"The level of work that P&G has entrusted to me is a real sign of belief in their employees. In three years, I have worked on several large lawsuits and acquisitions, with primary responsibility on some of those projects. I have had the opportunity to work on P&G's global business, which has provided me a terrific educational experience as well as some pretty interesting travel. In fact, while on a recent business trip to Japan, I was contacted by my management and asked to detour to Seoul to handle the legal negotiations for a Korean acquisition. P&G is such a large company with so many different types of business, there is always an opportunity and rarely a dull moment."

"Much of the work that even the most junior attorneys do is high profile. We see the advertising that we worked on (and changed the wording for!) while we're watching *Seinfeld* or reading *Time*. Many times, the transactions and cases we handle appear in the national news. We can also have a significant impact on the bottom line by challenging our competitors' misleading advertising, by negotiating a great contract, or by suing a company for copying one of our product's trade dress. It's definitely challenging and headline-making. The great thing about it is that we all support each other in that work. There's always someone to bat ideas around with, or someone who's worked on a similar issue and is willing to share their expertise."

Other Titles Available from Harcourt Brace

The National Directory Of Legal Employers

32,000 Great Job Openings For Law Students And Law School Graduates

The National Directory Of Legal Employers includes a universe of vital information about one thousand of the nation's top legal employers — in one convenient volume!

The National Directory Of Legal Employers includes the name of the hiring partner. The starting salary. How many people the firm intends to hire over the next year, and the criteria they'll use to choose successful candidates. The *Directory* also includes the specialties each firm practices, how the firms view their working environments, their achievements, their major clients, and their plans for the future.

Author: The National Association for Law Placement (NALP)
ISBN: 0-15-900380-6
Price: $39.95
(1,573 Pages, 8-1/2" x 11")

The Official Guide To Legal Specialties

With *The Official Guide To Legal Specialties* you'll get a behind-the-scenes glimpse at dozens of legal specialties. Not just lists of what to expect, real-life stories from top practitioners in each field. You'll learn exactly what it's like to be in some of America's most desirable professions. You'll get expert advice on what it takes to get a job in each field. How much you'll earn and what the day-to-day life is really like, the challenges you'll face, and the benefits you'll enjoy. With *The Official Guide To Legal Specialties* you'll have a wealth of information at your fingertips!

Author: The National Association for Law Placement (NALP)
ISBN: 0-15-900391-1
Price: $17.95
(Approx. 160 Pages, 6" x 9")

Includes the following specialties:

Admiralty	Environmental/Energy	Legislation
Antitrust	Government Practice	Product Liability
Appellate	Health Care	Public Finance
Bankruptcy	Immigration	Public Service
Communications	Insurance	Real Estate/Zoning
Corporate	Intellectual Property	Securities
Criminal	International	Sports
Domestic/Family	JAG	Tax
Entertainment	Labor/Employment	Trusts & Estates

CALL TO ORDER: 1-800-787-8717
ORDER ON-LINE: www.gilbertlaw.com

America's Greatest Places To Work With A Law Degree

And How To Make The Most Of Any Job, No Matter Where It Is!

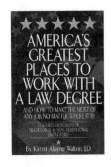

With *America's Greatest Places To Work With A Law Degree* you'll find out what it's really like to work at hundreds of terrific traditional and non-traditional employers – from fantastic law firms, to the Department of Justice, to great public interest employers, to corporate in-house counsel's offices, to dozens of others. You'll learn lots of sure-fire strategies for breaking into all kinds of desirable fields – like Sports, Entertainment, the Internet, and many,

Author: Kimm Alayne Walton, J.D.
ISBN: 0-15-900180-3
Price: $24.95
(1,146 Pages, 6" x 9")

many more. You'll discover the non-traditional field where new law school graduates pull down six figures – and love what they do! And you'll get hundreds of insider tips for making the most of your job, no matter WHERE you decide to work.

The bottom line is, no matter what you like, there's a dream job just waiting for you. Discover it in *America's Greatest Places To Work With A Law Degree.*

Beyond L.A. Law:

Stories Of People Who've Done Fascinating Things With A Law Degree

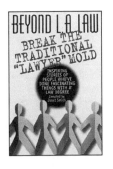

Anyone who watches television knows that being a lawyer means working your way up through a law firm — right?

Wrong!

Beyond L.A. Law gives you a fascinating glimpse into the lives of people who've broken the "lawyer" mold. They come from a variety of backgrounds — some had prior careers, others went straight through college and law school, and yet others have overcome poverty and physical handicaps. They got their degrees from all different kinds of law schools, all over the country. But they have one thing in common: they've all pursued their own, unique vision.

Author: The National Association for Law Placement (NALP)
ISBN: 0-15-900182-X
Price: $17.95
(192 Pages, 6" x 9")

As you read their stories, you'll see how they beat the odds to succeed. You'll learn career tips and strategies that work, from people who've put them to the test!

CALL TO ORDER: 1-800-787-8717
ORDER ON-LINE: www.gilbertlaw.com

Proceed With Caution

A Diary Of The First Year At One Of America's Largest, Most Prestigious Law Firms

Prestige. Famous clients. High-profile cases. Not to mention a starting salary approaching six figures.

It's not hard to figure out why so many law students dream of getting jobs at huge law firms. But when you strip away the glamour, what is it like to live that "dream"?

In *Proceed With Caution*, the author takes you behind the scenes, to show you what it's really like to be a junior associate at a huge law firm. After graduating from an Ivy League law school, he took a job as an associate with one of New York's blue-chip law firms.

Author: William F. Keates
ISBN: 0-15-900181-1
Price: $17.95
(166 Pages, 6" x 9", hardcover)

He also did something not many people do. He kept a diary, where he spelled out his day-to-day life at the firm in graphic detail.

Proceed With Caution excerpts the diary, from his first day at the firm to the day he quit.

What Lawyers Earn

And How To Negotiate For More!

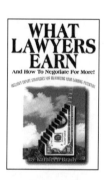

"Quality is remembered long after price is forgotten." This basic principle is the key to effective salary negotiation.

Think about it. Can you recall a "top of the line" purchase that outlived your expectations? Compare that to the "great bargain" purchase which fell apart as soon as you brought it home. Negotiating compensation is about these kinds of purchases. It is about convincing employers that you are "top of the line" merchandise, who will exceed their expectations and provide a return on their investment.

Author: Kathleen Brady
ISBN: 0-15-900183-8
Price: $19.95
(240 Pages, 6" x 9")

But how do you know what dollar figure indicates "top of the line?" How do you know exactly what you should ask for? How do you know what you are worth?

What Lawyers Earn answers these questions — and many more.

CALL TO ORDER: 1-800-787-8717
ORDER ON-LINE: www.gilbertlaw.com

Other Titles Available from Harcourt Brace

Guerrilla Tactics For Getting The Legal Job Of Your Dreams

Regardless of Your Grades, Your School, or Your Work Experience!

Whether you're looking for a summer clerkship or your first permanent job after law school, this national best-seller is the key to getting the legal job of your dreams.

Guerrilla Tactics for Getting the Legal Job of Your Dreams leads you step-by-step through everything you need to do to nail down that perfect job! You'll learn hundreds of simple-to-use strategies that will get you exactly where you want to go.

Author: Kimm Alayne Walton, J.D.
ISBN: 0-15-900317-2
Price: $24.95
(572 Pages, 6" x 9")

Guerrilla Tactics features the best strategies from some of the country's most innovative career advisors. The strategies in *Guerrilla Tactics* are so powerful that it even comes with a guarantee: Follow the advice in the book, and within one year of graduation you'll have the job of your dreams...or your money back!

Pick up a copy of *Guerrilla Tactics* today...and you'll be on your way to the job of your dreams!

CALL TO ORDER: 1-800-787-8717
ORDER ON-LINE: www.gilbertlaw.com

Notes